OSPREY MILITARY   **CAMPAIGN SERIES**   9

AGINCOURT 1415

GENERAL EDITOR DAVID G. CHANDLER

OSPREY MILITARY CAMPAIGN SERIES 9

AGINCOURT 1415

TRIUMPH AGAINST THE ODDS

MATTHEW BENNETT

◀ *Henry V preparing for battle at Agincourt. He wears full plate armour except for the head. A servant kneels with his open-faced bascinet while the king's body squire, John Cheyney, stands ready with the great helm circled by a golden crown. In the background a groom holds the head of the grey palfrey from which the king made his speech before the battle. The helmet, sword and saddle may still be seen in Westminster Abbey.*

First published in 1991 by Osprey
Publishing Ltd, 59 Grosvenor Street,
London W1X 9DA.
© Copyright 1991 Osprey Publishing
Ltd

*British Library Cataloguing in
Publication Data*
Bennett, Matthew
Agincourt 1415: triumph against the
odds.
1. Great Britain. France. Wars,
history, 1328-1498
I. Title
944.025
ISBN 1-85532-132-7

Produced by DAG Publications Ltd
for Osprey Publishing Ltd.

For a catalogue of all
books published by
Osprey Military, please
write to:
The Marketing Manager,
Consumer Catalogue
Department,
Osprey Publishing Ltd,
59 Grosvenor Street,
London W1X 9DA.

Colour bird's eye view illustrations by
Cilla Eurich.
Colour figure illustrations by Jeffrey
Burn.
Drawings based on manuscript
illustrations by V. Bennett.
Cartography by Micromap.
Wargaming Agincourt 1415 by Paul
Stevenson.
Wargames consultant Duncan
Macfarlane.
Typeset by Ronset Typesetters Ltd,
Darwen, Lancashire.
Mono camerawork by M&E
Reproductions, North Fambridge,
Essex.
Printed and bound in Hong Kong.

CONTENTS

Note: Many of the illustrations in this book have been drawn from contemporary manuscript pictures. References to retinues in the captions to the coats of arms provide two sets of numbers: those at the outset of the campaign; and (in parentheses) those present at the Battle of Agincourt.

Northern France and Southern England in the Early 15th Century

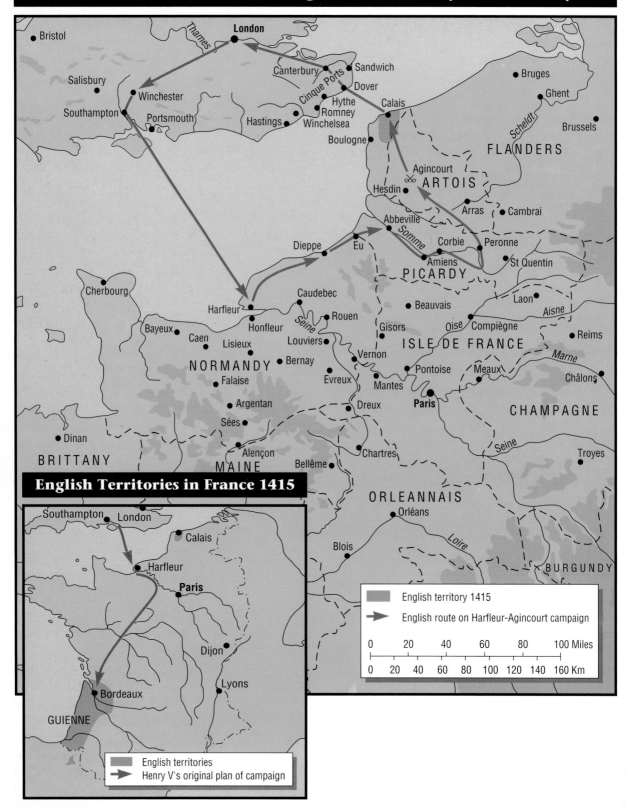

English Territories in France 1415

English territory 1415

English route on Harfleur-Agincourt campaign

| 0 | 20 | 40 | 60 | 80 | 100 Miles |

| 0 | 20 | 40 | 60 | 80 | 100 | 120 | 140 | 160 Km |

English territories

Henry V's original plan of campaign

ORIGINS OF THE BATTLE

On the evening of 24 October 1415, 28-year-old King Henry of England faced his greatest test. His small army was sick and exhausted and trapped by at least three times its number of fresh, confident French troops. Henry had tried to avoid fighting but he knew that next day it was inevitable. Against all expectations the battle that followed would turn out to be a decisive victory for the English, fought in a field near the village that was to give it its name – Agincourt.

At Agincourt, Henry V was fighting to recover what he believed to be his birthright: the Duchy of Normandy. This had last been in English hands more than two hundred years ago, before the French king took it from King John, his vassal. The intense rivalry between the French and English crowns dated back to 1066, when William the Bastard, Duke of Normandy, conquered England. But the dukes of Normandy had always been the vassals of the French Crown, and their elevation to royalty in one part of their realm did not change this relationship. In the mid-twelfth century the Norman kings were replaced by another dynasty, the counts of Anjou, who held extensive lands in the west and south-west of France. The new king, Henry II, actually ruled an 'empire' more powerful than that of his overlord. But his weak younger son, John, was not able to hold on to it in the face of a determined assault, both legal and military, by the French king, Philip II. In 1204, Normandy was overrun, England retaining only its possessions south of the River Loire. The minority of Henry III (1215-70) ushered in a period of political instability in England. This led to the disadvantageous Treaty of Paris in 1259, by which Henry gave up his rights to Normandy, Anjou and other territories, and agreed to do homage to the French king for his southern possessions of Aquitaine and Gascony. His son, Edward I (1270-1307), was a more

powerful ruler and wished to redress the balance in favour of England. But he was preoccupied with extending his power within the British Isles, and, apart from hostilities between 1294 and 1298, he made no attempt to enforce his claims against the French.

His reign was followed by another period of confusion when domestic concerns dominated English politics. A resurgent Scotland under Robert the Bruce inflicted a series of defeats, which led eventually to the deposition and murder of Edward II in 1327. There had been a brief conflict with France in 1324-5, known, after the town being fought over, as the War of Saint Sardos; but this was inconclusive. Edward III was only fifteen when he succeeded to the throne. In the following year the French king, Charles IV, died, leaving no male heir. Edward had a claim to the French throne through his mother, Charles's sister, but the French were not about to allow him to inherit. They invoked the Salic Law, an ancient custom that the crown should not pass through the female line. The French king's cousin, Philip of Valois, was the preferred choice, and – given the political and military situation at the time – there was nothing that Edward could do about it.

With every new reign the French king required homage for the English Crown's French possessions. This had been a problem since the beginning of the fourteenth century as it led to extensive legal wrangling, and homages had to be negotiated in rapid succession: in 1314, 1316, 1322 and now in 1328. The evident reluctance of Edward II to perform homage, aggravated by the conflict over Saint Sardos, meant that he only came into his Continental inheritance after paying £60,000 feudal 'relief' and handing over the territory of the Agenais. But it was his young son who actually performed homage to Charles IV. As king, Edward III performed homage twice more, in 1329 and

1331. Such ceremonies were far more than legal niceties. They helped to establish the justness of a ruler's cause should it come to war – and Philip VI had clear intentions to win England's rich southern French possessions. He devised an invasion plan for Gascony in 1329. The actual cause for war was Edward's refusal to hand over the renegade Count Robert of Artois, so that in 1337 Philip declared Gascony forfeit. Edward's response was to claim the French throne himself.

This is not the place to go into a detailed history of the ensuing conflict, now known as the Hundred Years War, up until 1415. Several issues need to be considered, however. English and French fortunes had fluctuated over the intervening eighty years. Edward's land campaigns in 1339 and 1340 were inconclusive, although a great victory was won at sea, off Sluys. The English

◄*Richard II knighting the 12-year-old Prince Henry in 1399 (the same year in which he became Prince of Wales). (Harl. MSS 1319)*

tactic was that of chevauchée, literally rides through French territory to inflict damage, win plunder and undermine Philip's authority. When Edward's force was caught at Crécy in 1346, and his son the Black Prince was trapped at Poitiers ten years later, they both inflicted signal defeats on the French. In 1356, King John and many of his nobles were actually captured, giving the English the upper hand in the subsequent ransom and territorial negotiations; these resulted in the Treaty of Bretigny in 1360, which assured Edward's possessions in western France, and some (excluding Normandy) in the north.

But in the same year a French fleet landed on the English coast, sacked and burned Winchelsea. This sort of destructive naval raid continued at intervals for the rest of the century. What is more, the English strategy of chevauchée began to fail.

▶ *Henry V armed cap-à-pie and mounted on his warhorse, from his chantry chapel in Westminster Abbey. This was how rulers liked to portray themselves, as warriors, in a self-glorifying style that bore no relation to the realities of war.*

The Dauphin, who became Charles V in 1364, advised by his wily Constable Bertrand du Guesclin, declined battle in favour of a 'scorched earth' policy. English raiders were harried through devastated land by French forces that would not stand and fight. In 1370, Sir Richard Knolles, and three years later, John of Gaunt, conducted expeditions that were humiliating failures. In 1375, the Truce of Bruges was established, and within two years both Edwards were dead, leaving a minor on the throne.

Richard II's reign was a troubled one, but he did have a genuine desire for peace, which was achieved for the last decade of the fourteenth century. Richard's overthrow and murder by Henry of Lancaster in 1399 changed the political situation again. French naval raids and attempted intervention in England were matched by English expeditions in 1405, 1410 and 1412. These were neither large nor particularly successful, however. In 1415 the English were looking back on a generation of defeats.

Three factors made Henry's invasion something more than a desperate gamble. One was the undoubted superiority of English arms in battle. English archers, if properly deployed, constituted one of the most formidable fighting forces in Europe. Second, in Henry they had a commander of energy and determination. Third, and most important, the French were riven by personal and political disputes that extended as far as civil war. Charles VI was insane, and in the absence of his authority, two groups of nobles, known as the Burgundians and the Armagnacs, vied for supremacy. It was this disunity that was to prove fatal for the French in the 1415 campaign.

◀ *The Royal Arms of England, quarterly 1&4 France Modern azure three fleurs de lis or, 2&3 gules 3 lions passant guardant or, borne by Henry V. The angels symbolize divine aid. Chantry chapel Westminster Abbey.*

▶ *Henry V, King of England. This modern reconstruction is based upon an early sixteenth century copy of a contemporary portrait. This is probably a good likeness and may be compared with a head carved in 1971 to restore Henry's tomb in Westminster Abbey. He was a handsome, well-built and athletic man, every inch a king, whom even his enemies respected.*

THE OPPOSING COMMANDERS

Henry V, King of England

The formal beginning to young Henry's military career was in 1399, when at the age of twelve, he was knighted. In fact he was knighted twice. On the first occasion this was by Richard II who had taken him that summer on his Irish campaign, as a hostage for his exiled father's good behaviour. He was then knighted again by his father, Henry Bolingbroke, the day before his coronation as Henry IV, having deposed Richard in a coup d'état. Twelve was an unusual, though not exceptionally early, age to be knighted. What was unusual, and what gave Henry an invaluable apprenticeship in the career of arms, were the circumstances of the usurpation that made the second knighting necessary. By deposing, im-

prisoning and later secretly murdering Richard, Henry IV had, whatever his justification, acted contrary to the laws of God and Man. This legitimized rebellion against his rule, and more than half his reign was spent in dealing with the results of his seizure of power.

The first campaign during which Henry saw service was against Scotland in 1400. Then, as Prince of Wales, he was faced with a full-scale and determined revolt by Owain Glendwr (who also claimed that title). The young prince was only the nominal leader at first, working with the powerful 'Marcher' lords who wielded effective power in the area. The Welsh used guerrilla tactics, relying upon raids and a swift retreat to mountain hideouts. So the 1402 campaign, when 'night after night the army lay in the open, drenched to the skin and half-starved' in pursuit of an elusive enemy, taught Henry the dreary realities of warfare. He also received military instruction from two members of the Percy family. Harry Hotspur was his first tutor; and in 1403 Thomas, Earl of Worcester, took over the role. Ironically, later in that year Henry was to face both of them in battle.

The Percies, with the Earl of Northumberland at their head, had helped Henry IV to the throne. Now the family wanted full control. So they made an alliance with Glendwr, and Percy forces marched to unite with him in the summer of 1403. By swift marching, King Henry was able to prevent their junction. At Shrewsbury, on 21 July, with Prince Henry leading the left wing, the rebels were soundly defeated. Hotspur was killed and his army dispersed. But it was a far from easy victory. The Royalists had to advance uphill into a hail of archery from some of the best bowmen in the kingdom, notably those of Cheshire. Young Henry was himself wounded in the face by an arrow, but bore the pain until victory was won. This was truly a baptism of fire. Henry proved his courage and determination in the teeth of the most fearsome tactical weapon of his time, one that he was to turn on the French a dozen years later.

Already Henry was unusual – he had a fought a battle. In fact he was to fight two in the twenty-odd years of his military career; Agincourt was the other. For battles were rare events at this time. Warfare was mainly given over to long sieges of castles and towns. Accordingly, the reconquest of Wales dragged on for another five years. In 1405 a great rebellion involving Glendwr, the Percies and the Mortimers was crushed at Bramham Moor, the Earl of Northumberland being killed. There was even a French expeditionary force landed at Milford Haven to link with the Welsh in a southern thrust; but it sailed home with nothing achieved.

So, when his father died in 1413, Henry was already an experienced warrior after a military education of the most harsh and practical kind. He had endured long marches in appalling weather conditions. He had suffered the tedium and discomfort of the siege-lines. As well as seeing many skirmishes, he had commanded men in formal, open battle. Above all, he had been taught the need for attention to detail in war. His preparations for the Agincourt campaign were massive and meticulous, to ensure the necessary numbers of men and sufficient amount of weaponry and ammunition.

In order to do this he needed about him men of competence and honesty. Bishop Henry Beaufort, his uncle, as well as providing or arranging the huge loans necessary to fund the expedition, oversaw the recruitment of his army. The Earl of Arundel, his treasurer, organized the payment of sailors and the provision of supplies for the voyage. The Earl of Dorset, his admiral, gathered together the invasion fleet. Richard Courtenay, Bishop of Norwich, was involved in diplomatic and intelligence-gathering activities (we know this because his agent in Paris was later arrested and tried for treason). Nicholas Merbury, Master of the Ordnance, provided ammunition and other equipment of war.

On campaign, Henry surrounded himself with experienced and trusted subordinates – for the most part. He also took with him Edward, Earl of March, who had been involved in the plot that was uncovered only a few days before the departure for France. Admittedly it was Edward himself who had confessed, but he was a dangerous man (his claim to the throne was in fact stronger than Henry's) and it is a mark of the King's confidence that he pardoned and continued to employ the Earl. For the rest, there were Humphrey, Duke of Gloucester, and Thomas, Duke of Clarence, the King's brothers; the Earls of Suffolk, Cambridge and Oxford; the Duke of York, the king's uncle; and numerous subordinates such as that old war-horse Sir Thomas Erpingham, the King's Steward; Sir John Holland and Sir John Cornwall. An important aspect of Henry's success as a leader was his ability to win respect from everyone, whatever their age or experience – and even from his enemies.

▼ *Humphrey, Duke of Gloucester; an exact copy of a contemporary sketch.*

In summary, Henry was the complete medieval military man and model king. This is not to say that he was perfect in all things. There is no doubt that he took his responsibilities very seriously. He had inherited rights in France, especially in Normandy, and he felt a responsibility to enforce them. Similarly, on the larger issue of the French crown, he had a family responsibility to his great-grandfather, Edward III, to achieve this, if possible. A very pious man, he was acutely aware of the sanctity of Church property and of his duty to his subjects. Accordingly, he strictly enforced ordinances controlling the behaviour of his troops on campaign. The discipline he demanded paid him back in full at Agincourt. In addition he possessed both moral and physical bravery; his confidence never appeared to be shaken even in such desperate circumstances as at Agincourt. Above all, he knew his trade as a soldier. He appreciated the

◀ *Michael de la Pole, Earl of Suffolk. Note the organization of plates around the face, and the protection for shoulder and elbow.*

▼ *Effigy of the Earl of Oxford, his head resting on his great helmet. Note the chain mail beneath the metal gorget and the roundel at the elbow.*

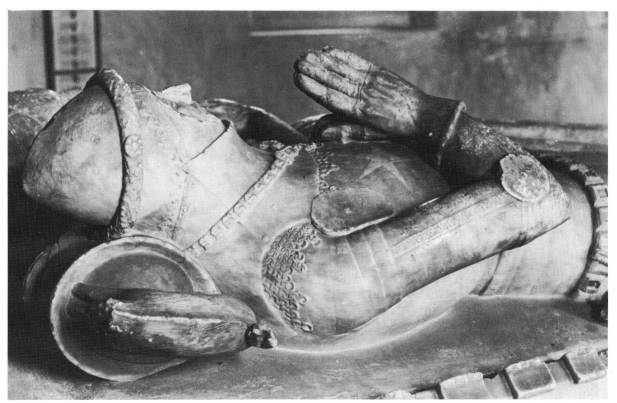

importance of the sea and the need for a strong fleet (although this was not created until after Agincourt). He accepted no bounds to the campaigning season and later was to prosecute what is known as the 'War of the Sieges' (1417-22), which firmly established his rule in Normandy, with unrivalled determination. Rouen, the province's capital, was taken after a seven-month siege (July 1418 to January 1419). Meaux took as long and this mostly in the winter months. It was after the capture of the town that he died, exhausted, probably of dysentery, that most common and disgusting of soldiers' diseases. His death, two months before that of Charles VI of France, meant that he never held the Joint Crown he strove for. He was a victim of his own success,

There is a side to his character little dwelt upon. French commentators noted that he was a harsh and arrogant man, assured of his own rectitude. His single-mindedness made him ruthless. And his ruthlessness made him cruel. It was this that made him hang prisoners after a siege. He oversaw a massacre at the taking of Caen in 1417. During the long siege of Rouen he refused food to the women and children expelled from the city and trapped between the siege-lines and the city walls. Technically he was within his rights according to the 'laws of war' at the time; but he need not have stuck to their letter. So it is with the massacre of the prisoners at Agincourt. He had justification for what he did, but it was a horrific act. Constant war from an early age had brutalized him. He was a cold and heartless warrior, which made a mighty king.

The French Commanders

In contrast to the English, who were led, as we have seen, by a commander of the first rank, the French were in a mess. Their king, Charles VI,

▲ *Charles VI, King of France, based upon his tomb effigy at St. Denis. He is shown wearing a remarkable gold parade helmet discovered in the courtyard of the Louvre in an old well in 1987. It is decorated with symbols of the French monarchy, notably the fleur de lis, and is encircled by his motto 'En bien', constantly repeated. This seems a suitable depiction of a king whose madness made him think he was made of glass, an unsatisfactory delusion for a soldier, and which made him incompetent to command in war.*

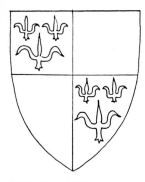

▲ *Charles d'Albret, Constable of France, arms quarterly 1&4 France Modern 2&3 gules. He was killed leading the first line at Agincourt.*

▶ *Charles d'Albret, Constable of France, stands beneath his banner in the first rank at Agincourt. He is dressed for combat, with a mail aventail and open-faced bascinet in preference to a heavy, vision-inhibiting closed helmet. He has drawn his sword and left off his scabbard, which could prove an encumbrance while fighting.*

◀ *The jupon or coat armour of Charles VI dating to the late fourteenth century and now in Chartres cathedral in perfect condition. It was originally a plain bright red.*

was subject to fits of insanity to which he had been victim for over twenty years. Despite his undoubted bravery and moments of sanity, he was unfit to command. His son, the Dauphin Louis, was an unhealthy and unmilitary lad of nineteen with no experience of war. This crucial weakness at the top had resulted in a situation of near civil war in which the Burgundian and Armagnac factions struggled for supremacy. In such a situation there was no possibility of undivided command.

The King (or his advisers) preferred not to call upon either John, Duke of Burgundy, or Charles, Duke of Orleans to lead the army. They could not work together: John had assassinated Charles's father in 1413 (and was to be murdered in revenge in 1419) while Burgundy was equivocal about whether to oppose the English or to ally themselves with them. John did allow his subjects to serve in the French army, but declined himself and forbade his son's presence.

Next in seniority came Charles, Duke of Orleans, aged only 24 and with little military experience; John, Duke of Bourbon, a 33-three year old who had won a victory over an Anglo-Gascon force during a chevauchée at Soubise in 1413; and John, Duke of Alençon, who, at thirty, had proved himself a failure as a military leader in the Bourges campaign three years earlier. They were asked to work in cooperation with the military officials of the Royal household: the Constable, Marshal and Master of the Crossbows.

In theory, this was a good solution. Charles d'Albret had held the post of Constable since 1402 and was an experienced and cautious warrior. John le Maingre, known as Boucicault, the Marshal, had an international reputation. A stalwart crusader, he had taken a leading part in the Burgundian Crusade so disastrously defeated at Nicopolis in 1396. Captured and ransomed from Sultan Bayezid, he had returned to defend Constantinople against Ottoman attack in 1399. He was already a hero of literature, his 'words and deeds' having been recorded in a book celebrating him as a model of chivalry. He was a legend in his own lifetime.

Had these two vastly experienced soldiers been able to exercise command, the result of King Henry's chevauchée might have been very different. For they advocated extreme caution: by avoiding battle and employing a 'scorched-earth' policy they planned to starve the English force into submission. They also devised a tactical plan by which the English might be defeated should it come to a fight. As we shall see, this was certainly the right strategy and these were probably the best tactics to employ. But when the day of battle came they were overruled by the arrogant young dukes, Princes of the Blood, over whom career soldiers such as they were could claim no authority.

D'Albret and Boucicault managed the campaign very well up to a few days before the battle. On the fateful day itself, if one were to ask who commanded the French army, the answer must be: no one. This, along with the evident, and contrasting, tactical competence and cohesion of the English, is the root cause of the French defeat.

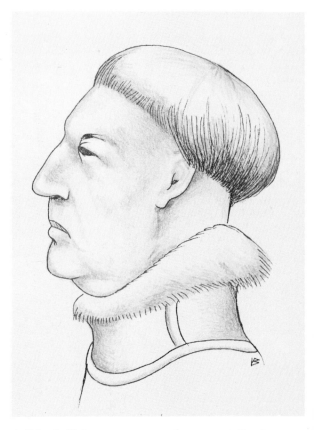

▲ *John le Maingre, Marshal Boucicault, from a contemporary portrait. This is the battered 'prizefighter's' face of a veteran* *of many wars fought over three decades. Boucicault advised avoiding battle with the English but was overruled.*

THE OPPOSING ARMIES

The Cavalry

Armies of the early fifteenth century were based on the man-at-arms: that is to say, someone clad in a complete suit of armour, trained to fight both on horse and foot. He could be a knight, if he possessed the necessary social standing and had undergone a formal ceremony; but more often he was not. While all important men were knights, many men-at-arms were simple esquires (the rank below and technically denoting a man suitable for knighting) or ordinary soldiers with no such pretensions. A man-at-arms was principally a cavalryman, by training and ethos, although, as we shall see, most fighting of the period was carried out on foot. He usually led a 'lance', a group of retainers who were also mounted, so he needed enough wealth to sustain the cost of several horses.

There were other types of cavalry, more lightly equipped, known since the time of Edward III as 'hobilars', although they played no role in the Agincourt campaign. A third to a half of English archers also rode horses, although they should be seen only as mounted infantry, gaining increasing mobility for the strategy of chevauchée.

The Infantry

The most common form of infantry soldier was the ordinary spearman. His weapon might be a halberd, with an axe-like head rather than a spear point, and he was armoured according to his means, usually with a helmet and brigandine. As well as filling the back ranks on the battlefield, his job involved the hard slog of siege work, which occupied so much of medieval campaigns.

The missile-men were of three types: archers, crossbowmen and gunners. The success of the

▶ *Arming a knight, from an early fifteenth century manuscript. As well as showing details of armour for man and horse, it makes the point that each man-at-arms needed the support of a team of servants to support him and his mounts – usually one or two warhorses, a riding horse for every member of the 'lance' and a packhorse.*

◀ French infantrymen. This French manuscript shows the kinds of soldiers provided by the urban communities. The equipment is varied: with bascinets and pot helms, more mail than a man-at-arms was wearing in 1415, and shields. The long shield on the left looks like a pavise, with a pointed base for holding it firm in the ground usually serving as protection for crossbowmen. Such shields were decorated with the coat of arms of the town.

▼ The Warwick Chamfron. Men-at-arms' horses were expected to be protected frontally, at least, to justify their rider's place in the battle line. At Agincourt it was as the cavalry charge was repulsed that the horses became maddened by arrows striking their unprotected flanks and rumps.

English longbow meant that archers habitually made up two-thirds of England's armies (and at Agincourt more than four-fifths). Their rapid shooting and destructive effect will be examined later. The French also possessed archers but did not use them so effectively. They relied more on the crossbow, which shot a heavier missile, or quarrel, but took much longer to reload. A crossbowman was usually accompanied by a companion bearing a large shield, a pavise, to protect them during reloading. This made the crossbow more useful in sieges than on the battlefield. The gunners, employed by both sides, were also more often engaged in siege work. There was already a wide range of types and sizes of artillery pieces, developed in the three-quarters of a century since their first appearance in Western Europe. They ranged from small, hand-held weapons to massive bombards used for battering down fortifications. It should be stressed that there was no proper, mobile, field artillery at the time of Agincourt.

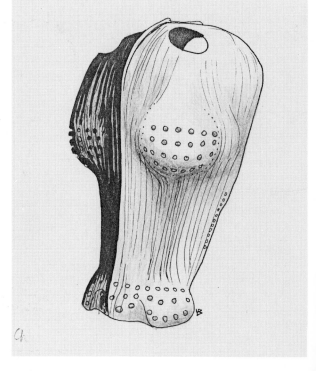

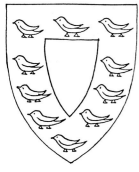

▲ *Sir Thomas Erpingham (b. 1357) KG 1401, arms vert an inescutcheon within an orle of martlets argent. An old warhorse, Steward of the King's Household, he commanded the archers at Agincourt. Retinue: 20 (16) men-at-arms, 60 (47) horsed archers.*

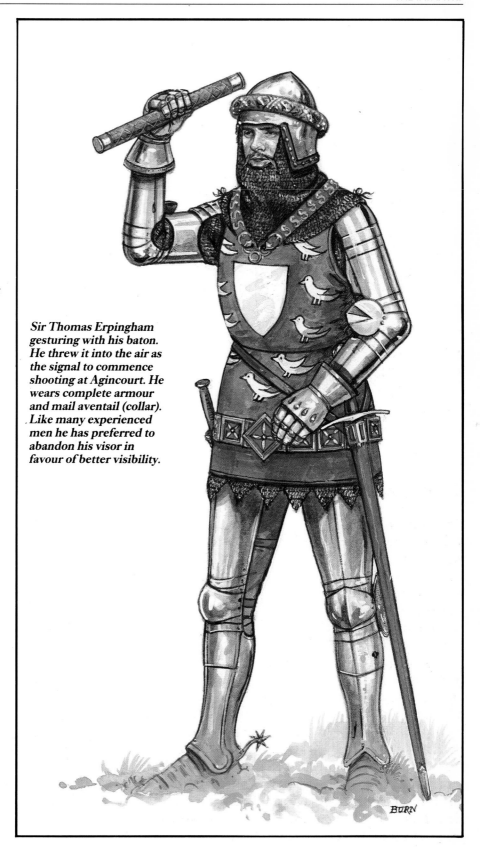

Sir Thomas Erpingham gesturing with his baton. He threw it into the air as the signal to commence shooting at Agincourt. He wears complete armour and mail aventail (collar). Like many experienced men he has preferred to abandon his visor in favour of better visibility.

The Man-at-Arms: Armour

Until the mid-thirteenth century, armour had been made of mail – closely interlocking rows of iron rings – but gradually pieces of steel were added to afford extra protection against blows and missiles. By 1415, the suit of plates, or complete armour, had almost reached its final state. A man-at-arms was covered 'cap-à-pied', from head-to-toe, in polished steel.

Under the armour a padded jerkin (akheton) was worn, both to prevent the metal rubbing and to absorb some of the force of an arrow. Until 1400 many men-at-arms wore a mail hauberk over this, and then a coat of plates. Such apparel was

▼*An early fifteenth century armour from the tomb of Fulk de Pembrugge IV, Tong church, Shropshire.*

undoubtedly heavy, but a greater problem was the threat of heat exhaustion under all that armour. The development of the complete 'white armour' (so-called because every piece was solid, polished metal) helped to alleviate this. No man could arm himself unaided; it needed at least one assistant. A complete suit was not impossibly heavy: at about 60-80lb (28-35kg), the weight of a complete harness did not exceed the load of a modern infantry pack. Furthermore, the weight was distri-buted around the body, each piece strapped on and articulated to suit the wearer's movements. So knights did not need to be lifted on to their horses by cranes as Olivier's film Henry V erroneously shows. A fit man could easily vault into the saddle.

▼A close-up of the Tong tomb, showing a bascinet with mail aventail, and the great helm supporting the figure's head.

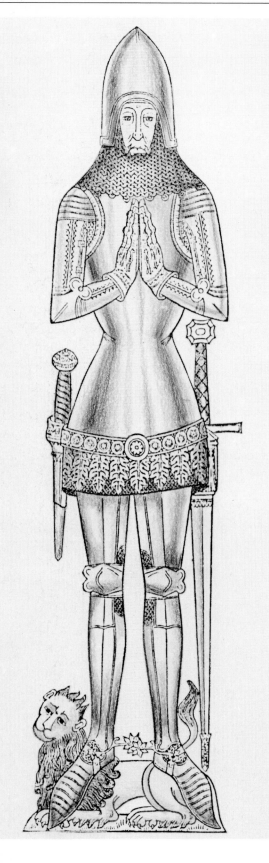

Nor were they unable to rise from a prostrate position, unless totally exhausted, stunned or otherwise injured.

The heaviest and probably most uncomfortable piece of armour was the helmet, and so it was the most frequently removed when action seemed distant or unlikely. The torso was covered by a back- and breast-plate hinged on the left side, buckled on the right and across the shoulders. The arms and legs had tubes similarly attached, elbow and knee covered respectively by 'couter' and 'poleyn' pieces to allow movement. Between waist and mid-thigh hung a skirt of hoops of steel (lames). Articulated gauntlets protected the hands and sabatons the feet. A recent development was the small, circular plate covering each armpit, a vulnerable area when the arm was raised for a

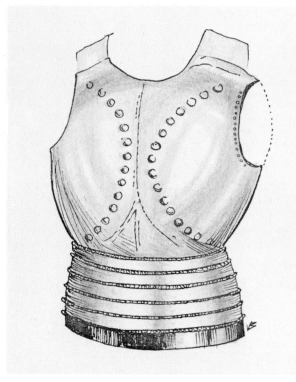

◄ *Brass of Sir Nicholas Dagworth at Blickling, Norfolk, 1401. This shows the style of armour worn at the beginning of the fifteenth century, featuring much chain mail, which was to reduce rapidly during Henry V's reign.*

▲ *A late fourteenth century breastplate and fauld (strips of armour below the waist) covered in cloth. This would be worn by a man-at-arms or possibly a wealthy crossbowman.*

blow. Another innovation, replacing the mail aventail, was a solid neck guard (gorget), which was attached to the helmet. This was known as the bascinet and was so ubiquitous that contemporaries used the term to denote men-at-arms (for example, 8,000 bascinets in the French van at Agincourt). It was close-fitting and sloped to a point at the back of the head. The face was protected either by a visor, or another helmet worn over it. The sharply-pointed visor gave rise to the term 'dog-faced bascinet' and could be hinged or slid open for better vision and ventilation. The bucket-like 'great helm' afforded neither comfort. It tended to be used in the tournament rather than in war, but Henry V wore one at Agincourt, and the double-protection it afforded probably saved his life.

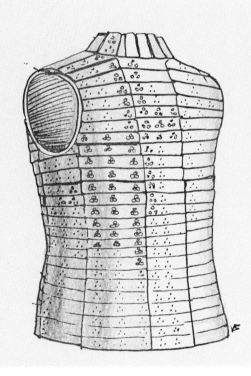

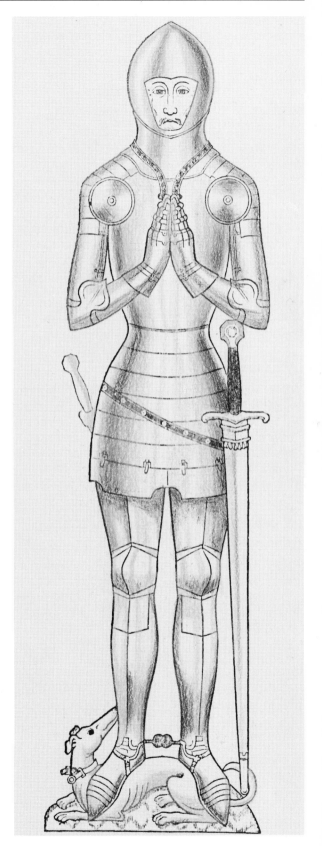

▲Brigandine. This was a common and cheaper form of armour than plate. It was covered in cloth so that only the rows of rivets showed on the surface. This example from the Musée de l'Armée in Paris shows its construction.

▶Brass of John Leventhorpe Esquire, in Sawbridgeworth Church, Hertfordshire, c.1433, illustrating armour typical of the latter period of Henry's reign, fully armoured with little visible chain mail.

Rich men had bands of brass or gilded brass to decorate their suits. Those with heraldic arms displayed them on a close-fitting garment called a 'cote d'armes' (literally, coat of arms). This made identification possible in battle and had great symbolic significance. When, a few days before Agincourt, Henry V vowed to wear his 'cote d'armes' at all times, he meant by this that he was constantly ready for battle. A late arrival at Agincourt actually improvised one from his trumpeter's banner. For the coat of arms also had the effect of declaring that its wearer was worth a ransom, a valuable insurance policy if threatened with death. It is commonly believed that the 'cote d'armes' was abandoned in the early fifteenth century, in favour of the all-steel 'white armour', but these two examples would seem to argue otherwise. Shields were falling out of fashion, so there was no other way of self-identification, and it is likely that all knights and nobles wore their 'cote d'armes' at Agincourt.

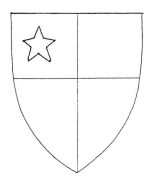

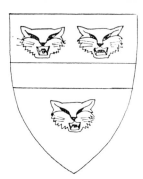

Coats of arms: two English examples.

▲*John de Vere, Earl of Oxford, arms quarterly gules and or in the first quarter a mullet argent. Joint rearguard commander with the Duke of York. Retinue: 40 (29) men-at-arms, 100 (79) foot archers.*

▲ *Michael de la Pole, Earl of Suffolk, arms azure a fess between three leopards' heads or. Michael senior died of dysentery at Harfleur, and was succeeded by his only son, also Michael, who was killed at Agincourt. Retinue: 40 (14) men-at-arms, 120 (44) horsed archers.*

▶ *An Italian great sword, c. 1400. This simple, functional, but beautiful weapon of about three feet in length (1m) was used by all types of soldiers.*

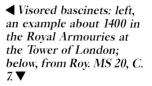

◀ *Visored bascinets: left, an example about 1400 in the Royal Armouries at the Tower of London; below, from Roy. MS 20, C. 7.* ▼

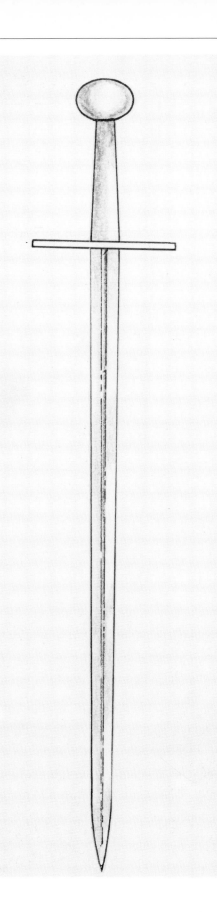

Other important items were the spurs, worn by all horsemen, but gilded in the case of knights to symbolize their higher status, These were removed for fighting on foot, as Henry V did.

The Man-at-Arms: Weapons

As a cavalryman, the man-at-arms learned to wield lance and sword. The lance was about 12 feet (4m) long, a stout piece of ash (usually) thickening towards the grip and with a long, slender point. On horseback it was tucked firmly under the arm while the legs were braced against stirrups and saddle, making man and horse a projectile to unhorse or pierce the armour of an opponent. On foot it was shortened by half to make it more wieldy. Increasingly favoured was the poleaxe, a wicked weapon with an axe-head on a four- to six-feet shaft bound with metal so that it could not be lopped off. It could used to bludgeon, transfix or cleave an opponent.

The queen of weapons was the sword – the symbol of knighthood and nobility. Made of the finest steel (that of Bordeaux was highly prized), most were some three feet long with a simple cross-guard and heavy pommel. Some specialist weapons were slim, with a diamond section, for piercing armour, but most had a broad, doubled-edged blade for cutting. Longer swords, wielded in both hands, were also popular (although they had not yet reached the monster proportions-of the sixteenth century). Finally, on his right hip the man-at-arms carried a dagger of 'ballock' or misericord style. Not really a combat weapon, it could be used to dispatch a wounded opponent, or as a last resort. It could slip through a visor or gaps in armour to wound or kill an otherwise invulnerable man.

Not all could afford the equipment described, but substantial numbers of men-at-arms were armed to this standard.

The Archer

Armour was not the primary concern of the archer; flexibility and mobility were. Accordingly, they wore either padded jerkins or brigandines (which contained metal plates) but little other body armour. The head was protected by an open-faced bascinet or the popular wide-brimmed 'pot-helm' and possibly a camail. Some leg or arm armour may have been worn, but the archers at Agincourt neglected even their breeches!

The archer's bow was a six-foot stave of elm, ash or preferably yew. The 'back' of the bow was flat and the 'belly' rounded, giving it a 'D' section

▶ *Practice with the bow. This well-known drawing from the mid-fourteenth century Luttrell Psalter shows how the English developed their battle-winning skills. The practice shafts are tipped with bulbous arrowheads, presumably a safety measure.*

◀ *An English archer at Agincourt. Standing behind the protection of the six-foot sharpened stakes, he is lightly armoured. On his head he wears a simple iron cap, and his body-armour is a brigandine. His half-hose and loin cloth, the only covering for his lower limbs, suggest that he is one of the many victims of dysentery in Henry's army.*

tapering to the nocks where the string was attached. The bow was usually kept unstrung with the string in a pouch to keep it dry. Stringing and unstringing took but a matter of seconds, allowing bowmen to pop the string under their hats should it come on to rain!

The English bow of this period is normally called a longbow, although it is not the description

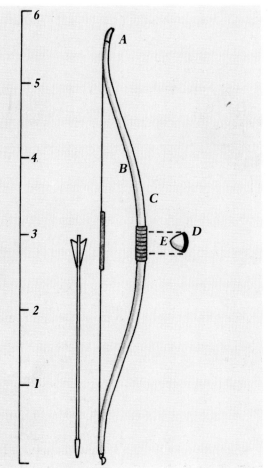

◀ The longbow, showing its construction. A, nock; B, belly; C, back; D, sapwood; E, hardwood. Approximate length just under six feet.

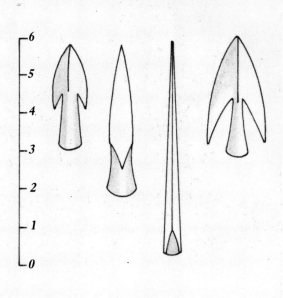

▼ Types of arrow heads. Left to right: general purpose, armour-piercing bodkin type, mail-piercing bodkin, hunting type used against unprotected horse. (Based on surviving examples in the Museum of London.) Scale in inches.

used by contemporaries. For it is not so much the length of the bow but its 'pull' (power) and the expertise of the user that matter. This could vary from 80lb up to 150lb, but to pull a bow of the latter magnitude required great strength and technique. Hence training from an early age was crucial, and English kings were able to promote the skill throughout their lands, giving them an invaluable pool of skilled archers. Although Edward III feared that the French might follow the English example, they never managed to do so. (This may be because the French monarchy feared to arm the lower classes effectively in case of rebellion.) The range of a longbow is often given as 400 yards (365m), but killing range was little more than half that, and real execution was not probably not achieved over 50 yards. But it is important to remember that the bow was not outdone in these respects until the mid-nineteenth century! Also, it was not necessary to kill the enemy: wounding and terrifying their horses or forcing them to retreat through fear of death would be enough for victory. Each archer carried as many as four dozen arrows in a quiver or in his waist-belt. The rate of shooting could reach up to ten or twelve arrows a minute. At close range, arrows could pierce the best armour, and the 'arrow-storm' was capable of driving back even the most determined opposition.

The Crossbowman

The crossbowman usually wore more armour than the archer. As a weapon in use at sieges, this, together with the large shield, might have been a necessary protection. Illustrations show body and leg armour in addition to the helmet. There are almost no contemporary illustrations for 1415, however; most cited as such date to half-a-century or more later. Furthermore many come from expensive manuscripts which represent battles and equipment in a highly stylized manner, so that missile-men appear as heavily armoured as the

◄*Crossbowmen. Loading the crossbow was a strenuous activity as these drawings show. The development of racheted devices to draw back the stiff string made it easier, but it was still a slow weapon to load and fire.*

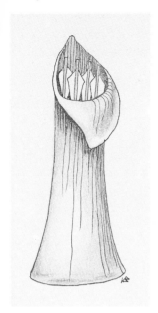

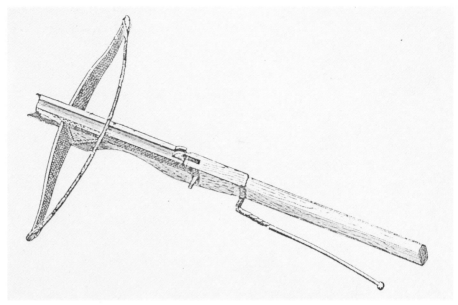

▲ *A crossbow and quiver, with bolts (shown at different scales).*

knights! Headgear was usually the pot-helm, although there existed a type of bascinet with a hinged flap on the right side of the face, which could be lifted when the butt was brought up to the face to aim and shoot.

The crossbow itself was a popular weapon among all ranks of society. It varied in size from the light hunting bow, often shot from horseback, to the heavy war bow. For this larger weapon the stave was about three feet (1m) long and had a butt of similar length. The bow was usually 'composite', made up of laminated layers of wood, bone and sinew. Steel bows were being introduced in the early fifteenth century. Crossbow quarrels or bolts were both shorter and heavier than those of an ordinary bow. These bolts were a foot to eighteen inches (30-45cm) in length and fletched with leather or wooden 'feathers'. About a dozen bolts were carried in a quiver worn on the waist-belt.

Heavy crossbows could outrange a longbow, but most had a similar carry of up to 400 yards. Although it could be shot on flat trajectory, crossbowmen also used high, falling fire to pierce helmets and shoulder armour. At short range it was unstoppable. Its weakness was its slow rate of fire. Although every bow had a 'stirrup' in which the user placed his foot in order to 'span' it, that is to draw the string back into shooting position, most crossbows needed some sort of spanning device. This might be as simple as a hook attached to a heavy belt, the string being drawn back into position as the wearer stood up. Or there was the cranequin or windlass, ratchet devices with a handle that was wound until the thick string was held by a rotating 'nut', set in the butt. This gave the advantage of keeping the weapon spanned until the shooter decided to loose at his target by squeezing the simple form of trigger. Loading was a laborious business though, and the rate of fire was limited to two or three a shots a minute.

The Gunner

The gunners' role during the Agincourt campaign was more to do with the siege of Harfleur than with the battle. Such men were specialists, and the masters of their profession had a Europe-wide reputation. Their main job was the transportation and operation of heavy bombards and siege guns. Accordingly they wore heavy siege armour (much as later engineers were to do) protecting head and chest. There was also a new breed of handgunner now appearing on the battlefield. Within a few years of Agincourt the Bohemian Hussites were to show how devastating a combination of artillery and handguns could be. The handgunner wore the

English mounted archer on the march. He wears an open-faced Italian-style bascinet, a stout brigandine, shooting gloves and tall riding boots. He carries his bow in a weatherproof bag and his arrows in a quiver with a protective cap. His whole equipment and his mount show him to be a well-off yeoman of the type who made a living out of war.

usual light armour of the missile-man and carried a metal tube fixed to a pole – his gun. To fire he brought a piece of slow-burning cord, or match, up to the touch-hole, either by hand or using a simple trigger like that of the crossbow.

We know that there were guns in the French army for the Agincourt campaign, although their size is not specified. It is unlikely that they were deployed for battle, however, as no eyewitness describes their actual use. The English suffered at least one casualty, an archer, to a gun, probably a hand weapon.

Organization: The English

In order to raise forces for the campaign, Henry relied upon the 'indenture' system. This was so called after the document that listed the knights' and soldiers' names. Indenture had replaced the earlier method of raising troops through feudal obligation in the reign of Edward III. Feudal service was limited to 40 days, which was inadequate for a campaign fought in France. So to raise troops the king effectively dealt with contractors. These were often his feudal vassals as well, great lords, knights and esquires, but they were serving for pay. So the King's brother, Humphrey, Duke of Gloucester, contracted to raise 200 lances (that is, men-at-arms with their servants) made up of himself, six knights, 193 esquires and 600 mounted archers. By the day of Agincourt, the rigours of campaigning had reduced them to 162 lances and 406 archers. A middle-ranking esquire such as Thomas Chaucer (the poet's son) provided 14 lances, 62 mounted and 60 foot archers (of which he could field 9 lances and 37 archers at the battle). At the lowest level, Lewis Robbesard, Esquire, brought along his tiny retinue of three foot archers.

The retinue, literally those retained or supported by their master, was the basic building block of the 'host' (as a medieval army should properly be called). Links of lordship meant that many lesser men were effectively under the command of their feudal superior.

The only other organizational division was into three bodies: the vanguard, centre and rearguard, in which the army marched and fought. In battle, men fought under the banner of their lord, who in turn looked to that of the commander of the 'battle' (the rather confusing medieval term for division) for direction. Command and control were weak in such an organization. There was no uniform system for giving oral commands (although the archers were told when to start shooting at Agincourt). Movement orders were given by shouting the battlecry and advancing the standards in the desired direction. This meant that battlefield manoeuvre on foot was a slow and cautious affair, in case the ranks should fall into confusion, something Henry proved himself very well aware of at Agincourt.

Organization: The French

Although it employed a similar system of *lettres de retenue* to raise and maintain troops, the French monarchy had not advanced nearly as far toward a contractual organization as had the English. The French tended to fight in their own territories, and often on the defensive, so there was not the need to develop this sort of machinery. Feudal service and the 'arrière ban' (literally, reserve call-up), a general obligation on every subject, sufficed. By the early fifteenth century the general levy had usually been replaced either by a cash payment, or by the provision of selected troops from the towns. Apparently, Paris offered to provide 6,000 crossbowmen and 'pavisiers' for the 1415 campaign, although these were turned down by the French commanders – the huge numbers of feudal tenants and their vassals who flocked to Rouen were considered sufficient for the task. In fact, gathering too large a host was a considerable logistical headache for the French. The experienced captains, such as Marshal Boucicault, preferred small, well-equipped and well-disciplined forces. Even so, many thousands of footmen drawn from the locality gathered at Ruisseauville just to the north of Agincourt, although they took no part in the battle.

The French command structure supposedly worked in the same way as did the English. In fact, as we shall see, it broke down completely, although not for lack of planning; rather through inept application.

ORDERS OF BATTLE

Unlike modern armies medieval hosts were composed of individuals and their followings. It is consequently a hit-or-miss affair as to whether records of agreements (indentures) survive. The work done by the nineteenth century antiquary Sir Harris Nicolas does provide some valuable information though. He provides two lists for the English forces, one for the campaign and another for Agincourt alone, when their numbers were much reduced. Neither can be considered as complete. Numbers of some individual contingents may be found under the coats-of-arms illustrating this book. Otherwise it is best to refer to Nicolas (pp. 333-89) for comprehensive details.

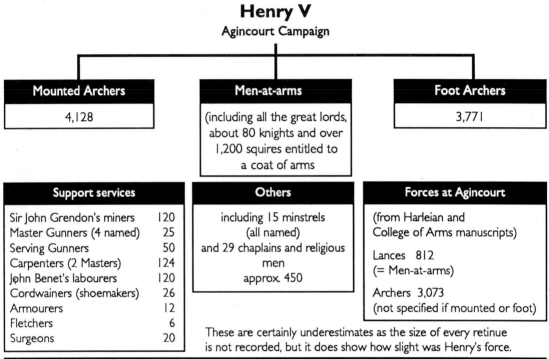

Henry V
Agincourt Campaign

Mounted Archers	Men-at-arms	Foot Archers
4,128	(including all the great lords, about 80 knights and over 1,200 squires entitled to a coat of arms	3,771

Support services		Others	Forces at Agincourt
Sir John Grendon's miners	120	including 15 minstrels (all named) and 29 chaplains and religious men approx. 450	(from Harleian and College of Arms manuscripts)
Master Gunners (4 named)	25		
Serving Gunners	50		Lances 812 (= Men-at-arms)
Carpenters (2 Masters)	124		
John Benet's labourers	120		Archers 3,073 (not specified if mounted or foot)
Cordwainers (shoemakers)	26		
Armourers	12		
Fletchers	6		
Surgeons	20		

These are certainly underestimates as the size of every retinue is not recorded, but it does show how slight was Henry's force.

French Army

Unfortunately no equivalent records survive for the French forces which requires reliance upon chroniclers' guesses.

A possible breakdown at Agincourt is:

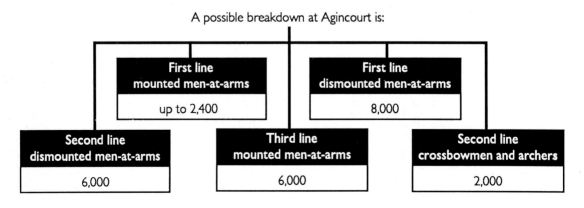

First line mounted men-at-arms	First line dismounted men-at-arms
up to 2,400	8,000

Second line dismounted men-at-arms	Third line mounted men-at-arms	Second line crossbowmen and archers
6,000	6,000	2,000

ENGLISH HERALDRY

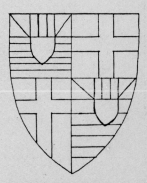

Edward, Duke of York, the King's uncle (b. 1373). *Royal arms differenced with a label of three points each charged with three roundels gules. A Knight of Garter (KG) from 1387, he had served in Wales and with Clarence in 1412. Killed at Agincourt. Retinue: 100 men-at-arms, 300 horsed archers.*

Thomas, Duke of Clarence, second son Henry IV (b. 1388). *Royal arms with a label azure of three points each charged with three ermine spots. He had campaigned in France in 1412 and played a major role at Harfleur from where he was invalided home. Retinue: 240 men-at-arms and 720 horsed archers.*

Humphrey, Duke of Gloucester, fourth son Henry IV (b. 1390). *Royal arms within a bordure argent. Severely wounded in the groin at Agincourt, King Henry may have saved his life. Retinue: 200 (142) men-at-arms, 600 (406) horsed archers.*

Edmund Mortimer, Earl of March, *arms quarterly 1&4 barry of six a chef paly and corners gyronny or and azure, an escutcheon argent 2&3 or cross gules. Invalided home from Harfleur. Retinue: 60 (29) men-at-arms, 160 (102) horsed archers.*

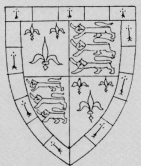

John Holland (later Earl of Huntingdon) *arms England with a bordure of France (azure seme of fleur de lis or). He distinguished himself at Harfleur. Retinue: 20 (16) men-at-arms, 60 (35) foot archers.*

Thomas Beaufort, Earl of Dorset, *Royal arms with a bordure compony (azure and ermine). Admiral of England, Ireland and Scotland, he was made Captain of Calais in 1413, and was left in charge of captured Harfleur with a garrison of 300 men-at-arms and 900 archers. His retinue of 100 men-at-arms and 300 horsed archers, however reduced by the siege, was probably included in this figure.*

John Mowbray, Earl Marshal, Earl of Nottingham (b. 1392) *arms England, a label of three points argent. Invalided home from Harfleur. Retinue: 50 (33) men-at-arms, 150 (80) horsed archers.*

Thomas Montagu, Earl of Salisbury (b. 1388) KG, *arms quarterly 1&4 argent three lozenges conjoined in fess gules, 2&3 or eagle displayed wings inverted vert. Retinue: 40 men-at-arms, 80 horsed archers.*

ENGLISH

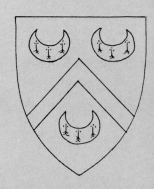

Sir John Cornwall KG 1409, arms ermine a lion rampant gules crowned or within a bordure sable bezantee. Henry's uncle by marriage, he was an old soldier with twenty-five years' experience and commanded the vanguard. Retinue: 30 men-at-arms, 90 foot archers.

Sir John Harington, arms sable fretty argent. Retinue: 30 (26) men-at-arms, 90 (86) horsed archers.

Sir John Grey, arms gules a lion rampant within a bordure engrailed argent. He helped repel the French sally which burnt the siege lines before the Leure gate at Harfleur. Retinue: 35 men-at-arms, 96 archers (at Agincourt).

Sir Robert Babthorp, arms sable a chevron or between three crescents ermine. Controller of the King's Household. Retinue: 5 (6) men-at-arms, 15 (18) foot archers.

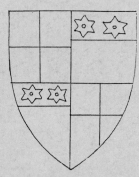

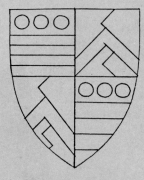

William, Baron Clinton, arms quarterly 1&4 sub-quarterly or and gules 2&3 argent on a chief azure two mullets pierced or. Retinue: 20 men-at-arms, 40 foot archers.

Thomas Strickland Esquire, arms sable three escallops argent. He bore the banner of St George at Agincourt. Retinue: 2 (1) men-at-arms, 6 (0) foot archers.

William, Baron Ferrers of Groby, arms gules seven mascules conjoined or. Retinue: 12 (5) men-at-arms, 36 (9) foot archers.

Sir Walter Hungerford, arms quarterly 1&4 sable two bars argent in chief three plates 2&3 per pale dancetty gules and vert a chevron or. The man with the unfortunate reputation for having voiced his desire for 10,000 more archers to King Henry on the eve of Agincourt. Retinue: 20 (17) men-at-arms, 60 (55) horsed archers.

HERALDRY

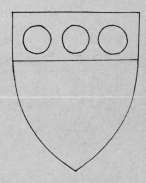

Sir Gilbert Umfraville (b. 1390) arms Gules crusilly and a cinqfoil or. A trusted contemporary of Henry, he was a Knight of the King's Chamber and led the advance guard. Retinue: 20 men-at-arms, 90 horsed archers.

Sir Gerard Ufflet, arms quarterly 1&4 or a bend between six martlets gules 2&3 argent on a fess azure three fleurs de lis or. Retinue: 20 (9) men-at-arms, 60 (33) horsed archers.

Gilbert, Baron Talbot (b. 1383) KG 1409 arms quarterly 1&4 gules a lion rampant within a bordure engrailed or 2&3 argent two lions passant in pale gules. He served under Henry as Prince of Wales. Retinue: 30 (20) men-at-arms, 90 (55) foot archers.

Thomas, Lord Camoys, a peer since 1383 KG 1415, arms or on a chief gules three roundels argent. A vastly experienced veteran, he had fought against the Scots, French and Welsh under Henry IV. He commanded the left wing at Agincourt. Retinue: 30 (24) men-at-arms, 60 (69) horsed archers.

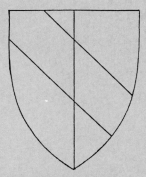

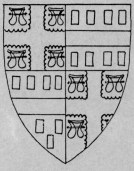

John, Baron Roos, arms gules three water-budgets argent. Retinue 20 (9) men-at-arms, 40 (22) foot archers.

John Cheyney, Esquire, arms quarterly 1&4 chequy or and azure a fess gules fretty ermine 2&3 or a lion rampant per fess gules and sable. Body-squire to the King. Retinue: 4 (4) men-at-arms, 12 (0) foot archers.

Thomas Chaucer, Esquire, arms party per pale agent and gules a bend countercharged. Son of Geoffrey Chaucer, civil servant and poet. Retinue: 12 (9) men-at-arms, 36 (37) horsed archers.

Sir William Bourchier, arms quarterly 1&4 argent a cross engrailed gules between four water-budgets sable 2&3 gules billettee or and a fess argent.

FRENCH

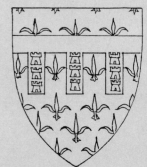

Charles, Duke of Orleans, arms France Modern (azure three fleurs de lis or) a label of three points argent. Taken prisoner at Agincourt.

John, Duke of Bourbon, arms France Modern a bend gules. Made a captive at Agincourt, he died in prison in England in 1433.

John, Duke of Alençon, arms France Modern on a bordure gules eight roundels argent. He led the second division at Agincourt and was killed in the mêlée, possibly by King Henry himself.

Charles of Artois, Count of Eu, arms France Ancient with a label of three points gules each charged with as many castles or. Taken prisoner at Agincourt.

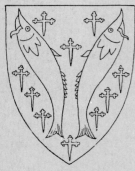

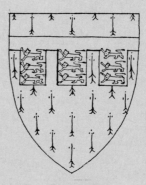

Edward, Duke of Bar, arms azure seme of cross-crosslets fitchee two barbels addorsed or. In the second division at Agincourt where he was killed.

Philip, Count of Nevers, arms France Modern a bordure compony gules and argent. A brother of John the Fearless, Duke of Burgundy, he was killed at Agincourt.

Arthur, Count of Richemont, arms ermine a label of three points charged with nine leopards or. He was taken prisoner at Agincourt and held until 1423.

Louis de Bourbon, son of the lord of Preaux, arms France Modern a bend and a bordure gules. He was killed at Agincourt, possibly while taking part in the left wing cavalry charge.

HERALDRY

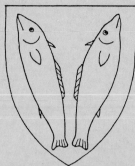

Louis, Count of Vendôme, arms quarterly 1&4 France Modern on a bend gules three lions rampant argent 2&3 argent a chief gules overall a lion rampant azure armed langued and crowned or. He commanded the left cavalry wing at Agincourt where he was taken prisoner by Sir John Cornwall.

Ferry de Lorraine, Count of Vaudemont, arms or on a bend gules three eagles displayed argent. He was in the main battle at Agincourt where he was killed.

Henry, Count of Blamont, arms gules two salmon addorsed argent. He fought in the main battle at Agincourt, where he was killed.

Jacques, Lord of Dampierre and Admiral of France, arms gules three pallets vair on a chief or two lions passant affronte sable. He fought and was killed in the front line at Agincourt.

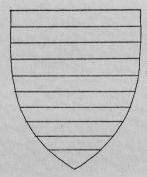

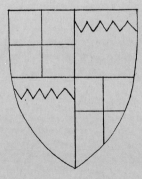

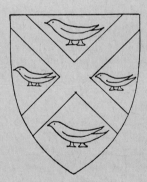

Robert, Count of Marle, arms azure a fleur de lis between two barbels addorsed. A commander of the third division at Agincourt who was killed in a final fruitless charge.

Edward, Count of Grandpre, arms barry of ten or and gules. He fought at Agincourt where he was killed.

John, Viscount Belliere, arms quarterly 1&4 subquarterly argent and sable 2&3 or a chief indented sable. He was in the left cavalry wing at Agincourt where he was killed.

John, Viscount of Breteuil, arms argent a saltire between four martlets gules. Captured at Agincourt.

THE AGINCOURT CAMPAIGN

As soon as he came to the throne, Henry V began preparing the ground for an invasion of France. He made overtures to Charles VI about marrying his daughter, Katherine. Embassies were exchanged in an attempt to find a settlement of English claims in France that would suit both sides, and in early 1415 there was an English delegation in Paris. As late as June that year, French ambassadors arrived in London. But Henry was not leaving everything to negotiation. The previous summer he had tried to arrange a military alliance with the Duke of Burgundy, specifying numbers of troops and a division of the Armagnac lords' territories as spoils. But this came to nothing. Justifiably perhaps, neither side could trust the other enough to seal an agreement.

While all this diplomatic activity was going on, Henry was rapidly, relentlessly and extensively preparing for war. Nicholas Merbury, Master of the Ordnance, had been instructed to stock up with bow staves and arrows in the summer of 1413. Already new guns were being cast in London and Bristol, and other siege equipment was being constructed: bowers, ladders and battering devices. Ships to transport the army and all its impedimenta were also being built and, from the spring of 1415, requisitioned, irrespective of nationality, for the crossing.

When he decided to invade, Henry gathered an army of some 2,500 men-at-arms and 8,000 archers. Since each 'lance' implied the presence of two to four horses for the man-at-arms and his body servants, and since half the archers were mounted, over 10,000 horses also required passage. Add to this, two hundred specialist gunners and non-combatants perhaps adding up to 1,000 altogether, and all the siege equipment, and it is apparent that a large fleet was essential. A chronicler's figure of 1,500 vessels is often accepted, although this was intended to impress rather than to record exact numbers. If the fleet was one fifth this size, or about 300 vessels, it was still ten times larger than Henry's standing 'navy' in 1417, and so a mightily impressive collection of ships.

The Siege of Harfleur

Negotiations having broken down, Henry mustered his army at Southampton in July. After a short delay spent dealing with an attempted coup d'état by some disaffected members of his court, the fleet set sail on 11 August. The King's flagship the *Trinité Royale*, a huge vessel of 500 tons and the largest in the fleet, gave the signal for the crossing. Henry kept the destination a secret until the last minute, and two nights later his ships rested at anchor in the estuary of the Seine. Henry held a council of war aboard his flagship and postponed landing until the next morning.

He had chosen Harfleur to be another Calais for the English. It was one of the 'keys of Normandy': once taken, it would give him access to the heart of 'his' duchy. But it was no easy nut to crack. It had strong walls, surmounted by 26 towers, and the defenders had broken the sluices in order to surround it by water. Its three gates were all guarded by barbicans, projecting defences of timber and earthwork. Two gates were already protected by water, leaving only the south-western gate possible to assault. Here the barbican was the most impressive: huge baulks of timber had been bound together by iron bands and almost matched the height of the walls. One chronicler asserts that it was a 'stone's throw' across. A channel led into the centre of the town where its port was situated, but this was blocked by a chain and wooden stakes to hole shipping. John, Lord of Estuteville, who commanded the defenders, had only a hundred men-at-arms and soldiers but was confident in the

The Agincourt Campaign

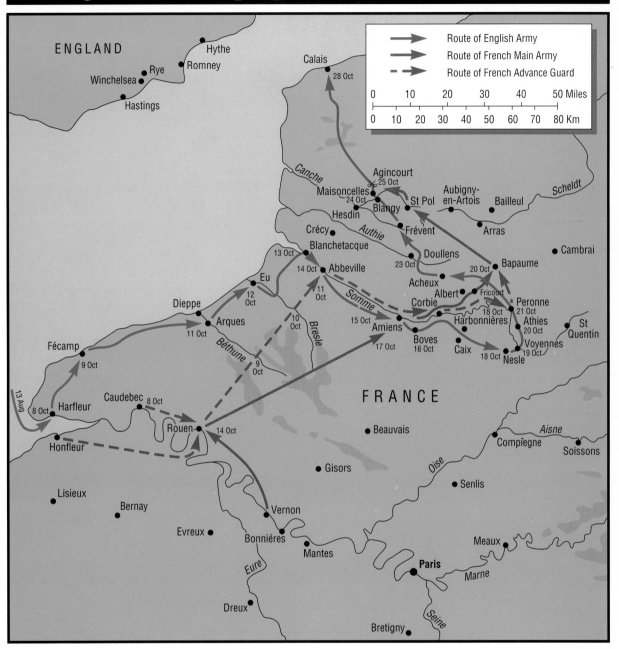

Route of English Army
Route of French Main Army
Route of French Advance Guard

strength of the town's defences.

The English took two days to disembark, Henry setting up camp opposite the main gate. He declared an ordinance that laid down standards of behaviour for the campaign. Looting, burning and molesting the civilian population were forbidden, and every Englishman was to identify himself by a red cross of St George. Since Henry claimed to be

recovering his lands he could not allow the normal destructive behaviour of his soldiers to take place. Necessary foraging was still allowed, especially for the horses, but any transgression of the rules was to be punished by hanging the culprit. It was Henry's firm and impartial application of the letter of his law that made him so respected.

The town could not be considered properly

invested until it had been surrounded. So, on the 18th, the Duke of Clarence led part of the army to set up camp on the far, eastern side of the town. In so doing he captured a French relief convoy bearing supplies of guns, powder, arrows and crossbows. He narrowly missed intercepting reinforcements under Ralph, son of the Lord of Gaucourt, though. De Gaucourt got into Harfleur with another 300 men, and they, together with his inspired leadership, undoubtedly contributed to extending the length of the siege.

The odds were overwhelming, but Henry's siege engineers were by no means optimistic of a rapid victory. His fears were justified. Attempts at mining and driving trenches up to the foot of the walls were frustrated by the flooded ditches or energetic French countermining. Greater reliance had therefore to be placed upon the artillery barrage. This was not all gunpowder artillery, many stone-throwing engines still being in use. The cast-iron guns, with their huge noise and the capacity to throw projectiles weighing up to a quarter of a ton, nevertheless inspired most fear. Many of the stone balls sent crashing into the walls and houses of Harfleur were also made into incendiary devices by adding burning tar. The lie of the ground, which allowed the defenders to overlook them, and determined sallies by de Gaucourt's men, made the gunners' task a far from easy one however. English casualties were heavy both from the long-range fire of French guns and crossbows and the garrison's sallies.

A detailed chronology of the siege is difficult to establish. By 3 September, in a letter to Bordeaux, Henry expressed confidence that he would have won the town and be on his way to Paris in another week. He was to be proved wrong.

◀Monumental brass of Sir John Fitzwaryn in Wantage Church, Berkshire, 1414. The gorget has no underlying layer of chain mail, and there are free-hanging rings along the edge of the mail skirt, possibly forming part of an edge of brass or gilded links.

▶Right, monumental brass of a knight of the D'Eresby family in Spilsby Church, Lincolnshire, about 1410. Note the fashionable wreath on the bascinet.
▶Far right: Brass of 1426 in Merevale Church, Warwickshire, assigned to Robert Lord Ferrers.

On the same day the Dauphin received a messenger who had slipped out of Harfleur. Despite this the French seem to have made no real effort to relieve the place. Only one chronicler mentions a failed cavalry attack, which resulted in no more than a skirmish and the French being driven off with ease. The real danger to the English soon appeared, though – disease. Dysentery appeared and spread rapidly through the army. The causes are not hard to find: the heat of midsummer, the filth of the siege-lines, foul water and probably the

▲ English gunners and gun at Harfleur. This piece, a bombard known as a 'fowler', is some nine feet in length and with a bore of one foot. It is breech-loading and fired a stone ball.

shell-fish of the estuary consumed in large quantities by the besiegers. No one was spared it; even the highest nobles, the Earls of Suffolk and March fell ill. Thomas Courtenay, Bishop of Norwich, contracted the disease, described as a 'bloody flux' on the 10th, and five days later he was dead. The ordinary soldiery must have suffered similarly.

The Siege of Harfleur

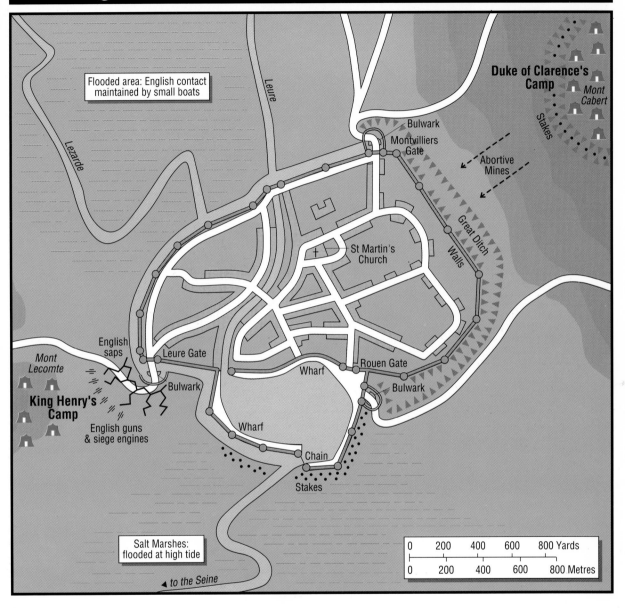

Flooded area: English contact maintained by small boats

Leure

Lezarde

Duke of Clarence's Camp

Mont Cabert

Stakes

Bulwark

Montvilliers Gate

Abortive Mines

Great Ditch

Walls

St Martin's Church

English saps

Leure Gate

Mont Lecomte

King Henry's Camp

English guns & siege engines

Bulwark

Wharf

Rouen Gate

Bulwark

Wharf

Chain

Stakes

Salt Marshes: flooded at high tide

to the Seine

| 0 | 200 | 400 | 600 | 800 Yards |
| 0 | 200 | 400 | 600 | 800 Metres |

Also on the 15th a French sally took and burnt the siege castle opposite the main gate. Then English luck changed. On the following day, John Holland led an attack on the main bastion, almost destroyed by bombardment, and captured it. This loss was crucial to the defenders. There was no longer any way of preventing the English from bringing up their guns to blast a breach in the walls. De Gaucourt offered to negotiate.

On Tuesday 17 September, the French agreed that if aid did not come from the King or Dauphin by midday on the following Sunday, they would surrender. This was according to the laws of war and spared the town a sack. The chance of looting was exactly what many Englishmen desired, but Henry agreed to the terms. No relief being forthcoming, he entered the town on Monday 23rd. Harfleur had been won, but at what cost? The siege had lasted five weeks. Over 2,000 men were dead from dysentery, including the Earl of Suffolk and many other notables. A large number, perhaps another 2,000 including the Duke of

Clarence, had to be sent home to recuperate. After Henry had appointed the Earl of Dorset to command a garrison of possibly as many as 500 men-at-arms and 1,000 archers, he had only 900 men-at-arms and less than 5,000 archers with which to continue the campaign. His letter to Bordeaux had envisaged a great chevauchée south to that city; now he had to content himself with more moderate objectives.

First he challenged the Dauphin to settle the issue by personal combat. This was not something that the sickly Louis was likely to accept, but Henry's motives were not entirely cynical. William Bruges, Guienne Herald and de Gaucourt set out on the 27th carrying the message. After the prescribed week had elapsed with no response, Henry thought again. Against all the wishes of his war council he decided to show the flag and march to Calais.

The March to Calais

On Monday 8 October, Henry's small force set out from Harfleur. It had a week's rations. This should have been enough for the hundred-mile march to Calais, but things were not to turn out as the English king had intended.

The French had seemed almost supinely inactive while Henry prosecuted the siege of a place described as 'a key to Normandy'. The problem was one of weak leadership. Charles VI, though keen to fight, was in a delicate state of mental health. His court was still riven by the discord between the Armagnac and Burgundian parties. The most suitable commander for the French host was undoubtedly John the Fearless, Duke of Burgundy, but for political reasons he was

◀ *Monumental brass of Sir Thomas de St. Quintin in Harpham Church, Yorkshire, about 1420. The bascinet features a curiously ornamental wreath representing a cluster of gems and a circle of feathers.*

▶ *Right: latten effigy of Sir John Wylcotes in Great Tew Church, Oxfordshire,*

1410. Note the large gussets of plate to provide protection for the armpits.

▶ *Far right: Latten effigy of Sir Thomas Braunflet in Wymington Church, Bedfordshire, 1430, illustrating the rapidly changing styles at the end of Henry's reign, with more completely plate armour and little mail.*

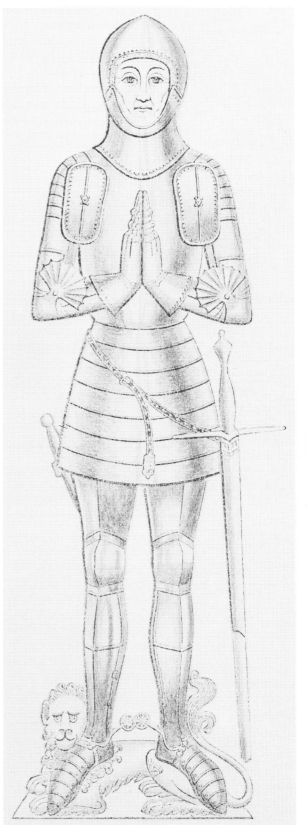

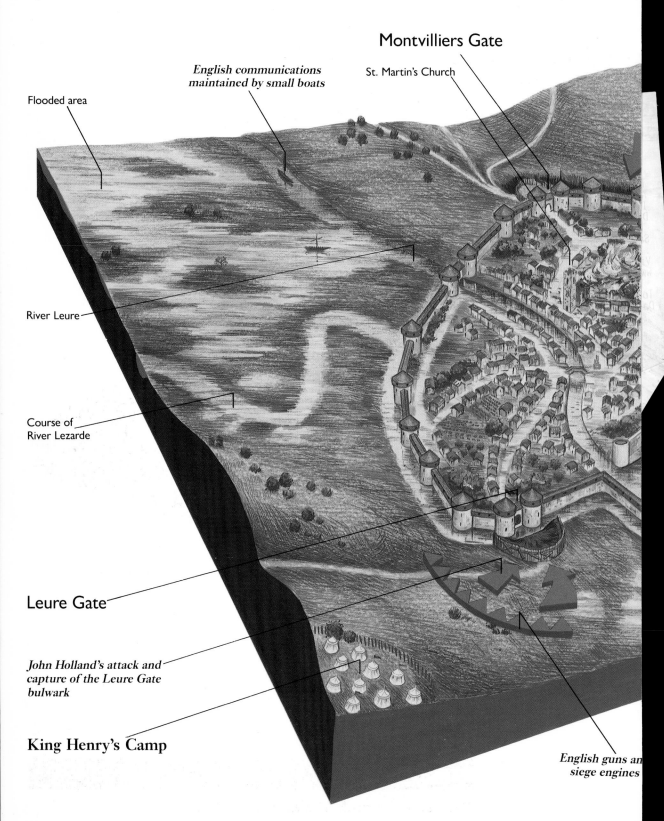

Montvilliers Gate

St. Martin's Church

English communications maintained by small boats

Flooded area

River Leure

Course of River Lezarde

Leure Gate

John Holland's attack and capture of the Leure Gate bulwark

King Henry's Camp

English guns an siege engines

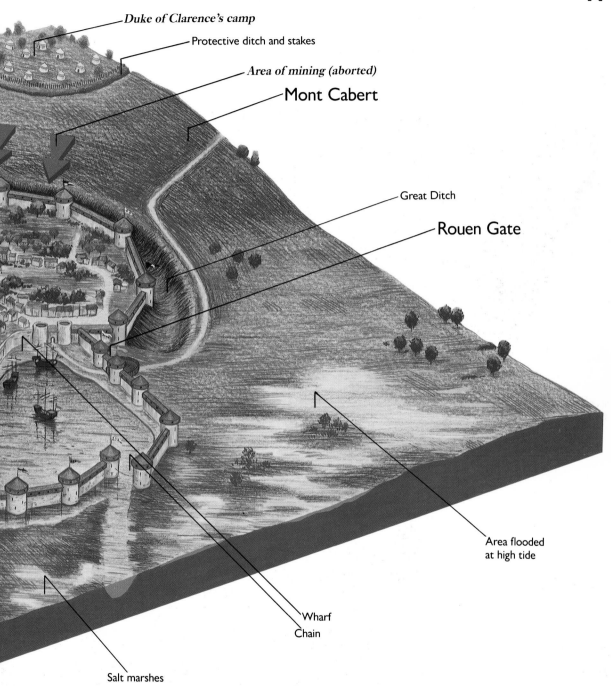

Duke of Clarence's camp

Protective ditch and stakes

Area of mining (aborted)

Mont Cabert

Great Ditch

Rouen Gate

Area flooded
at high tide

Wharf
Chain

Salt marshes

HARFLEUR

The decisive attack, 17 September 1415.

excluded 'from the court, from Paris and from the army'. As a result, although he expressed his willingness to lead the French forces against the invader, he stood aloof. In the past, French historians have blamed John the Fearless almost solely for the defeat at Agincourt, merely by reason of his absence. He has also been accused of ordering his vassals not to attend the muster to which their king had summoned them. This is not the case, and many did fight at Agincourt. He did prevent his son Philip from joining the host though, despite the young man's tears of rage and humiliation, but this may be seen as intelligent caution. War, whatever the poets made of it, was a dangerous occupation, not so much from enemy action as from the risk of disease. The English had already learned this bitter lesson at Harfleur. Also John was unwilling to entrust his son and heir to the Armagnac camp. Their leader, the ancient Duc de Berry, was far from enthusiastic about engaging the English in battle. He had been at Poitiers sixty years before, where his father, King John, had been taken prisoner. Accordingly he made quite sure that King Charles was not risked in a similar encounter. He did grudgingly agree that the English could be tackled, but only with the cynical comment: 'It is better to lose a battle than the king and a battle.'

King Charles raised the war standard at St Denis on 10 September, almost a month after the English had landed. He moved to Mantes, while the Dauphin, Louis, had already been established for a week at Vernon, on the borders of Normandy, in order to keep an eye on English movements. The Marshal, Boucicaut, may already have been at Caudebec, some 30 miles east of Harfleur, while the Constable, d'Albret, kept watch across the Seine estuary from Honfleur.

None of the experienced French commanders was keen to engage the English in battle. Their strategy was one of containment. After Henry set out, Boucicault shadowed his forces as they made for the ford of Blanchetacque to cross the Somme. Meanwhile d'Albret marched swiftly north-east from Rouen with the bulk of the French advance guard to organize the blocking of all passages over the river. The English advanced along the coastal route. Sir Gilbert Umfraville and Sir John Corn-wall led the van; the King, the Duke of Gloucester and John Holland (later Earl of Huntingdon) commanded the main body, while the Duke of York and the Earl of Oxford were in charge of the rearguard. The march passed without incident for the first three days, although French contemporaries accuse the English of sacking Fécamp. At Arques, on the 11th, the army encountered its first real resistance. The castellan refused to allow the English to take sustenance but soon caved in when Henry threatened to burn the town. It is unclear just how much the French had pursued a 'scorched earth' policy, but if they had, Henry must have been aware of the danger the supply situation posed. There was another skirmish at Eu the following day. Once again the English took the supplies they needed.

No Passage of the Somme

On the 13th, Henry continued his advance towards the ford of Blanchetacque, to take his forces across the mouth of the Somme. But a few miles before reaching the estuary the vanguard took a Gascon prisoner. He informed his captors that Constable d'Albret was at Abbeville with a force 6,000 strong. Furthermore the ford for which they were heading was blocked with stakes and guarded by troops under Guichard Dauphin, Lord of Jaligny . The English must have been dumbfounded. They were already half-way through their supplies, and there was as yet no obvious passage over the Somme. The only course of action was to turn south and march upriver, hoping to find a crossing that was undefended or that could be forced. Gloomier spirits considered that it might be necessary to travel as far as the river's headwaters, some sixty miles distant. Henry's course of action had proved as rash as his advisors had warned him. Here they were, caught 'like sheep in a fold' in their words: outnumbered, sick and running short of supplies in a hostile countryside.

Henry first led his force to Pont St Rèmy and then, finding the bridge defended, into billets in Bailleul and surrounding villages. The 14th saw similar fruitless efforts to find a passage. The English spent the night in and around Hangest.

Next day they arrived opposite Amiens and probably spent the night at Pont de Metz.

The French had been very thorough about destroying bridges and defending all crossing points, which suggests a well-organized, pre-determined plan. (Henry could make no attempt on a city the size of Amiens, of course. His force was too small and lacked siege weapons.) The itinerary of the French army is more difficult to identify than that of the English, but, as we have seen, it was divided into two bodies. The advance guard, under d'Albret and Boucicault, had already performed its role well. Perhaps getting news of Henry's intended movements, the Constable had taken the larger part of this force directly to Abbeville on the Somme. From a position between Harfleur and Rouen it would have taken some four days marching to achieve this, which suggests he moved at least as soon as Henry set out on the 8th. Perhaps the French utilized the time after the fall of Harfleur, while Henry waited fruitlessly for the Dauphin to respond to his offer of personal combat, to make their preparations.

It is not clear when the main body at Rouen, reckoned by chroniclers at 14,000 men-at-arms, also marched north. King Charles arrived at the city on the 12th and held a Great Council. Allowing some time for decision-making and organizing the large forces at his disposal, it is unlikely that the main body set out for Amiens before the 14th or 15th. Any earlier and it would have bumped into the English moving south at Amiens; any later and it could not have reached Bapaume, twenty miles north of Amiens, by the 20th when it is recorded as being there. This means that it probably arrived at Amiens on the 17th or 18th, crossing the path of the English army, which had by-passed the city a couple of days earlier.

From Pont de Metz to Boves, where Henry spent the night of the 16th, is only a short march of some nine or ten miles. It is not clear why Henry slowed his march at this point. Lack of supplies could have been the reason, though. The army had

▶ *The knightly surcoat or tabard of arms, worn over the armour. It was fashionable to wear the* *hair closely cut, often with small forked beard and moustache.*

by now exhausted the food it had brought from Harfleur. And it became apparent that there was no opportunity to cross the Somme. An eyewitness in the English army, known as the Chaplain, had gloomily predicted the French strategy: 'We then expected nothing else, but that after having finished our week's provisions and consumed our food, the enemy by craftily hastening on ahead and laying waste the country before us, would weaken us by famine . . . and overthrow us who were so very few, and wearied with much fatigue, and weak from lack of food.'

At Boves, Henry parleyed with the castle garrison. In return for not burning the town and its vineyards he demanded bread. This he received, eight baskets each needing two men to carry them, according to one source. Such provisions were essential to keep up the armies strength. Something also found in abundance at Boves was wine. The effect of a generous distribution of alcohol to men with empty stomachs could have been disastrous to discipline (which may have been the intention of the French). Henry forbade the common soldiery to take any more. When asked why they could not fill their water bottles, he replied that they would 'make bottles of their bellies' and get out of control.

Henry Raises Morale

That anecdote contains a message. Our sources only hint at the English morale at this time, but it must have been very low. Marching upriver away from Calais, unable owing to the marshy ground that lay between them even to get at their enemies who guarded the crossing points, reduced to subsisting on nuts and berries, and with no outcome in view except disgraceful death or capture at the hands of the French, many must have despaired. Surprisingly, perhaps, there is no mention of desertion. This may be because Henry still had his men firmly in hand, or that they feared the revenge of the French peasantry. The King's response in this situation is typical of his grasp of military psychology.

The next day (17th) he turned north to Corbie, which lay on the Somme. Perhaps he was trying to force a crossing, but perhaps he wanted a fight to

boost his men's morale. This he achieved, for the French garrison sallied out and there was a brisk skirmish. A later source asserts that it was here that John Bromley of Bromley, Staffordshire, performed a deed of great bravery. His kinsman, Sir Hugh Stafford, Lord Bourchier, bore the standard of Guienne. During a determined French assault this was torn from his grasp. But John Bromley hurled himself into the enemy ranks and, striking down the Frenchman who had captured it, recovered the banner. In later centuries this would have won him a medal. His family historian asserts that he was later allowed to add the arms of Guienne, a gold leopard on a red ground, to his own. This story is unproven – it may be no more than an edifying legend – but it is the kind of thing that happened in the countless small skirmishes of

▶ *The River Somme at Voyennes, one of the two crossing points for Henry's troops on 19 October 1415. The dimpling of the water surface in the centre of the picture shows where the water is still only knee-deep.*

medieval warfare. Such an exploit could hardly fail to raise morale and assure the English army of its man-for-man superiority when it came to fighting.

There is additional explanation for Henry's movements on the 17th, which also marks his skill as a commander. From his camp at Boves there was nothing to suggest that he was not going to continue along the left bank of the Somme. His attack on Corbie was designed to persuade the French that he intended to force a crossing. In fact he had no such intention. He had already decided to cut across the great loop of the river between Corbie and Ham, seeking an undefended passage. Perhaps he knew that the French advance guard was in Peronne, on the farthest point of this loop; we cannot be sure. Henry seemed to have some knowledge of French plans, for it was now that he

ordered each archer to prepare a six-foot stake, sharpened at each end, as a defence against cavalry attack.

Across the Somme

The English spent the night in the Caix-Harbonnières region, half way to their destination. On the 18th they advanced to near Nesle, only a couple of miles from the river. The Chaplain considers it 'the will of God' that news was brought to the King of a suitable crossing point. I consider that Henry was aware of the fact and intended to cross by the fords of Voyennes and Bethencourt. The English commenced this early the next day. At about eight o'clock on the morning of the 19th (first light?), they advanced into the

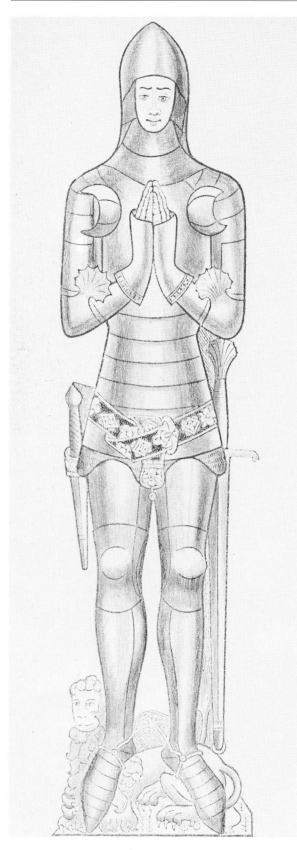

mile-wide marsh lying beside the river, The Chaplain speaks nervously of the army being caught in this vulnerable position, trapped between the Somme and a stream that fed it; but no enemy appeared. Two narrow causeways stretched over to the other side; they had both been broken down in the middle by the French. The Somme was about a couple of hundred yards wide at this point, but mainly marshy and only knee- to waist-deep. Part of the advance guard under Sir Gilbert Umfraville and Sir John Cornwall, a few horsemen and a mixture of spear- and bow-armed footmen splashed through these shallows to secure a bridgehead. But there was only space on the causeways for one horseman at a time, so the English set to work to repair them. Straw, fascines (bundles of sticks) and wood from various sources, including that torn from nearby buildings, was used to make a pathway wide enough to take three horses abreast. The main force began crossing about midday. So fearful was Henry that discipline might break down among his overstretched men that he personally regulated the flow of men and horses on one causeway, while two trusted subordinates watched the other. The risk of men pressing on too quickly for safety, or of panic spreading at the news of a supposed French assault, could so easily have reduced the crossing to chaos.

The French did, in fact, react to the English move. Soon after the advance guard was over the river, it was attacked by horsemen coming from the nearby villages. These were probably the outposts of the advance guard based at Peronne, quartered in outlying villages. That there was no coordinated response is clear. Later French chroniclers blame the men of St Quentin for not properly guarding the fords or making them impassable. Henry had succeeded brilliantly in slipping his bedraggled force across the river before the French could react. His whole army was over 'an hour before nightfall' (about five o'clock). He did not allow his jubilant men to rest, but advanced, even after it

◀ *Brass of a knight in South Kelsey Church, Lincolnshire, about 1420. The chain-mail skirt is escalloped, and the* *gauntlets are unusual in being protected each by a single piece of plate. The military belt is richly ornamented.*

▲ *The church at Athies, the village around which Henry rested his army on 20 October, expecting to be attacked by the French.*

grew dark, to Athies, where he made camp. The change of mood in the English army is well-chronicled by the Chaplain: 'We spent a joyful night in the nearby hamlets, from which, when we first started crossing the river, the French had emerged; and we rejoiced that we had, as many estimated, shortened our march by about a week. And we firmly hoped that the enemy host, which was said to be waiting for us at the head of the river would not wish to follow us and give battle.'

Where were the French?

Once again the clerical author is being naive. If the main French army was indeed at the head of the river, a day or two's march to the east, then the way was clear to Calais. Unfortunately, it was not. Where then, was the main body? It is usually assumed that it was in the vicinity of Peronne. Athies lies barely seven miles from Peronne - half a day's march away. Several modern commentators note the fact and the supposed imminence of battle. The challenge to battle sent by the Dukes of Bourbon and Orleans by three heralds on the 20th seems to confirm the fact. But the French did not offer battle that day. Instead they retreated to Bapaume, a long day's march to the north. Modern historians find this inexplicable. One explanation advanced is that they expected Henry to take the northern route to Calais and hoped to intercept him at Aubigny-en-Artois, between Arras and St Pol. This is certainly plausible although it does pose the question as to why the French host, three to four times greater in numbers than its opponent, should make this sudden and abject retreat. What is more, the English were now trapped, with their backs to the river they had just crossed. It is far more likely that it was only the advance guard at Peronne, roughly equivalent to or slightly smaller in numbers than the English. This had probably reached Peronne on the 18th, following the skirmish at Corbie, and had then lost touch with the enemy, who had struck south to Nesle. Next day it was too late to prevent the crossing, of course.

What, meanwhile, of the main body? As we have seen, this did not reach Amiens until the 17th at the earliest. It was also a very large force. Including camp followers, it could have numbered 50,000. In this case the riverbank route taken by the advance guard, whose job it was to watch the enemy closely anyway, was quite unsuitable. The roads were winding and the banks of the Somme swampy, especially with the heavy rains of that October. A more practicable route for a large force, encumbered with wagons and surplus personnel, was Bapaume, a couple of days to the north. Furthermore, the area around Peronne was not suitable for quartering a large force with its many horses. Villages were few and the terrain marshy. Bapaume, on the other hand, offered adequate facilities as well as being well placed to counter any English move to the north-west. At this time the French still expected that Henry would be forced to march to the head waters of the Somme, east of St Quentin. It might then have been necessary to move towards Cambrai, for which, once again, Bapaume was perfectly placed. If we accept that the French main body had moved directly to Bapaume, it makes French behaviour easily explicable. The French advance guard did

not wish to fight the English alone. It did have a contingency plan drawn up should this prove necessary. A recently discovered document (which will be discussed in detail later) provides us with a battle-plan drawn up by the commanders of the force to defeat the English by outflanking tactics. But once the English were across the river it was preferable to fall back on the main body. The French did mean to fight - but not yet.

Henry did not know that, of course. His reply to the heralds' challenge was that he intended to march straight to Calais. From then on he wore his coat armour at all times, a symbol of his preparation for battle at any moment. The English made no move on the 20th. It was a valuable rest day after the hectic marching and rapid crossing of the Somme. Also, Henry may have been expecting attack. Indeed it is possible that the French challenge was intended to pin him in place while the advance guard made its withdrawal. The situation suited both sides.

The March to Agincourt

Setting out once more on the 21st, the English army passed Peronne to the left. French cavalry came out to skirmish, but when the English horse drew up to oppose them fled back into the town. About a mile farther on, the Chaplain records that they crossed the tracks of a huge host – a stark

▲John le Maingre, de Boucicault, Marshal of France, arms argent a double-headed eagle displayed gules armed and membered azure. He was a veteran, knighted at the battle of Roosbeeke in 1382, and appointed Marshal in 1391. He was dragged wounded from a pile of corpses at Agincourt, made prisoner and died unransomed in England in 1421.

◀The castle at Peronne. The town was the base for the French advance guard and strategically sited above a bend in the Somme. Peronne was much damaged in the First World War; the original towers are shortened and now linked by a brick curtain wall.

Jean le Maingre, called Boucicault, Marshal of France. Advancing in full armour with his visor raised for better visibility, his neck and face are protected by a bevor. As a weapon he has chosen the fearsome poleaxe, a combined spear and axehead, murderous in close combat.

◀ *Warfare imagined – the joust. This was how the chivalrous classes liked to see themselves in warfare. (Misericord)*

▶ *The reality of warfare – troops pillaging. Destruction of property and persecution of the civilian population were the main ways of waging war. They undermined an enemy's political authority and could force him to offer battle to restore it.*

◀*Warfare imagined – the mounted mêlée. Serried ranks of well-equipped men-at-arms fight with chivalrous weapons to advertise their skills and add to their honour.*

▶ *The reality of warfare – logistics and movement. Unless engaged in a siege, it was better to keep troops on the move to help with supply. Horses and technical skills, represented here by a pontoon bridge, were essential for mobility.*

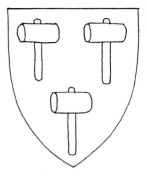

Guillaume de Martel, Sire de Bacqueveille, bearing the Oriflamme standard. This sacred banner, which signified war to the death, was ceremonially taken from its sanctuary at the royal abbey of Saint-Denis at the beginning of the Agincourt campaign. In fact, it was he who died, and the banner was lost in the press.

▲ William Martel (the Hammer) Lord of Bacqueville, arms or three hammers gules. He was authorized to bear the oriflamme, the Royal war-standard, on 28 March 1414. He was carrying it eighteen months later at Agincourt when he was killed.

reminder of the odds they faced. The army spent the night in the Mametz-Fricourt area. The French followed a parallel route some ten miles farther north-east. On the 22nd the English route was via Albert (then known as Ancre) as far as Forceville and Acheux. The French, who were ahead of their opponents, probably reached Coullement. On the 23rd the English pressed on past Doullens to Bonniéres and Frevent, while the French reached St Pol. The River Ternoise lay ahead and Henry intended to cross it at Blangy. This he achieved, although sources vary as to whether this was done unopposed or after a fight to preserve the bridge. While the crossing was taking place, Henry's scouts informed him that the enemy lay only a couple of miles to his right. Advancing in three battles the French drew up within half-a-mile of the English, who equally formed battle-order. But there was to be no battle that day. The French moved off northwards to Agincourt and Ruisseauville, where they encamped for the night. Henry followed up cautiously, fearing that they intended to move around the woods to his left front and attack him in the flank. But such was not their intention. The huge French host sat squarely across the Calais road. Henry took up quarters in the village of Maisoncelles. His army huddled around its few houses exposed to the teeming rain with only the gardens and orchards for cover. Barely a mile to the north the French built large fires and set guards to alert them should the English try to slip away in the night. From their well-lit camp, according to English sources, came the sound of the many horse and body servants of the French host attending to their duties, while the English played music to raise their spirits. So convinced were many of the English that they would meet their deaths the next day, that they confessed their sins, received the sacrament and made their peace with God.

▼ *The River Ternoise at Blangy. Some sources suggest that the English had to force a crossing here. It was from the ridge in the background that they first saw the huge French army moving across their path.*

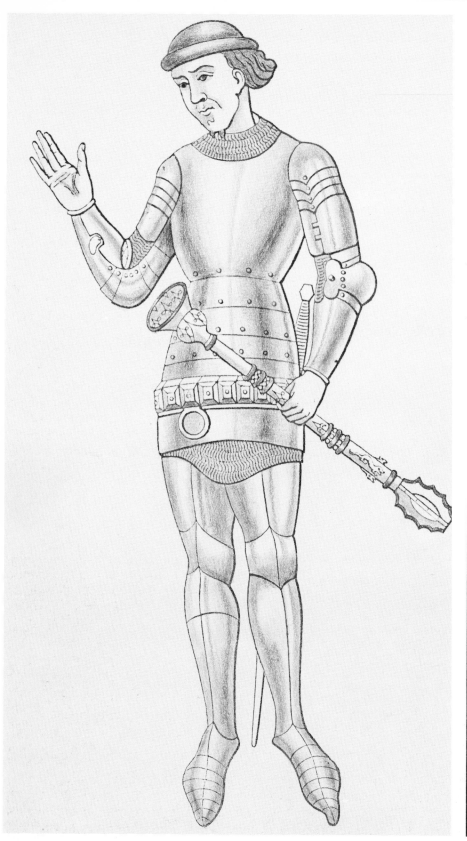

◀ *A serjeant-at-arms, from a slab in the church of St. Denis, about 1420. His mace, symbol of his rank, would have been of silver with enamel decoration.*

▼ *The battlefield, looking from the English camp at Maisoncelle. The fighting took place between the two woods in the background, about a mile away.*

THE BATTLE OF AGINCOURT

For the battle itself we are fortunate in possessing no less than four eyewitness accounts. This is good for any battle, but for the medieval period it is extraordinary. Furthermore, these were two of the participants on each side. In the English camp stood one of Henry's chaplains, from whom we have heard already, and in the battle line Jean le Fevre, Lord of St Rèmy. St Rèmy also knew many people in the French host and drew on their information when he came to write his chronicle.

Accompanying the French army were Enguerrand de Monstrelet and Waurin (both historians later patronized by the Burgundian dukes).

There are in addition several important secondary sources that contribute to our understanding of what happened. On the English side two chronicles draw largely on the Chaplain's 'Life'; while for the French, Pierre de Fenin and Juvenal des Ursins provide views that set the battle in a wider political context. The Duke of Welling-

▲ *The battlefield, looking from the French centre to their right flank. The woods were thicker in the fifteenth century, and Agincourt castle stood in the centre where the trees are thinnest.*

◀ *A mêlée illustrating the variety of weapons – swords, polearms and a war hammer – wielded by men-at-arms.*

ton was always scornful of attempts to reconstruct a battle, considering it as ephemeral as the goings on at a ball. But with many witnesses to corroborate the order of events it is possible to draw a pretty accurate picture.

More than this, the recent discovery by a young researcher of a vital manuscript in the British Library gives us an insight usually denied to historians. It is nothing less than the French plan of battle for the Agincourt campaign, outlining the deployment and tactics by which they hoped to defeat the English. As such it is not unique – a Burgundian battle plan exists from two years later – but it is very rare, and it allows us to reconstruct the battle as never before. Until now the English side of events has been easy to explain, the French

less so. Because of the importance of this discovery, the document will be explained and printed in full and then related to the actual events.

The French Battle Plan

It seems clear that the plan was drawn up for use by Marshal Boucicault and Constable d'Albret, who commanded the French advance guard. As we have seen, d'Albret had moved his force from Honfleur to Abbeville and had been joined there on the 13th by Boucicault's force, which previously had been harassing the English advance. Other leaders mentioned by chroniclers as present were: the Count of Vendôme, the Lord of Dampierre, the Duke of Alençon, the Count of Richemont

Agincourt: The French Plan

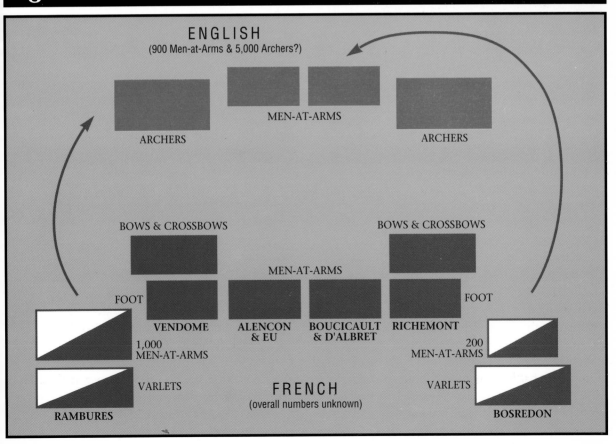

ENGLISH
(900 Men-at-Arms & 5,000 Archers?)

MEN-AT-ARMS

ARCHERS

ARCHERS

BOWS & CROSSBOWS

BOWS & CROSSBOWS

MEN-AT-ARMS

FOOT

FOOT

VENDOME

ALENCON
& EU

BOUCICAULT
& D'ALBRET

RICHEMONT

1,000
MEN-AT-ARMS

200
MEN-AT-ARMS

VARLETS

VARLETS

RAMBURES

FRENCH
(overall numbers unknown)

BOSREDON

(accompanied by the Lord of Combourg and Bertrand de Montauban, who had been with him at the siege of Parthenay) and David Rambures, the Master of Crossbows. Meanwhile, Guichard Dauphin, Lord of Jaligny was defending Blanchetacque. All these men (save Dampierre) are mentioned in the battle plan. Two other named lords, the Count of Eu and Louis de Bosredon are also known to have commanded in the campaign. In addition to Dampierre, the names of Clignet de Brébant and the Bastard of Bourbon are omitted. These were principal characters in the accounts of the time, and it surprising that they are not mentioned. Perhaps they are included under the heading of 'the other lords who are not named elsewhere' (para 4).

The advance guard was only some 6,000 strong, a number equal to or slightly less than that of the English. This may explain why it envisages using men not usually involved in battle, the varlets who accompanied their masters, the men-at-arms, to look after their needs, horses and equipment. The plan may have drawn up at any time from 13 October to the 20th, when the advanced guard joined the main body at Bapaume. It could have been intended to deal with the English should they have got across the Somme at any time on their march southwards from Blanchetacque. Alternatively it need not have been drawn up until the 19th, when the advance guard at Peronne became aware that the English had indeed crossed the river. As we have seen, despite a challenge to battle on the 20th, nothing actually took place, with the French advance guard retiring safely upon the main body. It may be significant that Henry apparently became aware of the French intention to use cavalry against his archers on about 17 October, although this does not mean that the plan was completed or that the English had more than an inkling of it.

It is noticeable that many aspects of the plan seem to have been put into operation at Agincourt, although the increased numbers of the French host made it impracticable – and in fact contributed to the disaster. What follows, though, is a very shrewd set of tactics designed to neutralize and defeat the main English weapon, their archers. (The symbols after a lord's name indicates his fate at Agincourt: + for killed and P for taken prisoner.)

The French Plan

'This is what seems best to the Lord Marshal [Boucicault] (P) and the lords with him, by the command of the Dukes of Alençon (+) and Richemont (P) and the Lord Constable [d'Albret] (+) for the instruction of the said lords in the conduct of battle.

'First, in the name of God, Our Lady and Saint George, it is advised that they make up a large Battle [division] to serve as the vanguard in which there will be the Lord Constable and the Lord Marshal, with all their men. In this Battle the banners of the Lord Constable and the Lord Marshal should be together, with that of the Lord Constable on the right side and that of the Lord Marshal to the left side. And on the right side should be all the men of the Lord Constable and on the left side all the men of the Lord Marshal.

'There is to be another battle next to this one, in which there will be the Duke of Alençon, the Count of Eu (+) and the other lords who are not named elsewhere. And if the English form up in one Battle these battles should be together, so they may all join together.

'It appears necessary to form two large wings of foot. The Lord of Richemont is to organize one of these, which shall be the right; and there will be in his company, aside from his men, the Lord of Combourg (+) and Lord Bertrand de Montauban (+); and the other, which will be the left, the Lord of Vendôme, the Grand Master of the King's Household (P) is to organize, together with the Lord of Jaligny (+).

[Damaged: 'There shall be?] the axes of the company and others who can be found elsewhere [Damaged: behind / to the side of / together with] the above two wings. [This is tantalising, but unclear: were there to be separate bodies of axe/polearm-wielding infantry?]

'The missile-men [*gens de trait*] of the whole company will stand in front of the two wings of foot, where the knights and squires shall arrange them, each to his own side.

'Have a large battle of horses belonging to noblemen up to the number of one thousand men-

FRENCH HERALDRY

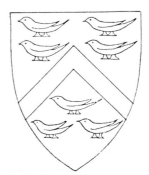

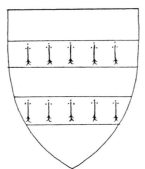

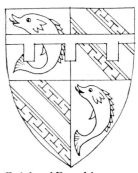

Jacques, Lord of Crequy, Marshal of Guienne, arms or a crequier plant eradicated gules. Taken prisoner and killed at Agincourt.

Robert, Lord of Beaumesnil, arms gules two bars ermine. Killed at Agincourt.

John, Lord of Aumont, 'the Brawler', arms argent a chevron between seven martlets gules (4 & 3). He was in the left cavalry wing at Agincourt where he was killed.

Guichard Dauphin, Lord of Jaligny, Grand Master of the King's Household (disputed with Vendôme) arms quarterly 1&4 or a dolphin embowed azure 2&3 azure a bend argent double-cotised potent-counterpart or overall a label of three points gules. He played a prominent part in the campaign blocking the ford at Blanchetacque and fighting in the main battle at Agincourt, where he was killed.

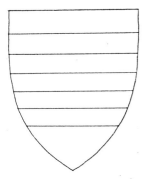

David, Lord of Rambures, Grand Master of the Crossbowmen (since 1412) arms or three bars gules. He fought in the main battle at Agincourt where he was killed along with three of his four sons.

John, Count of Roucy, arms or a lion rampant azure armed and langued gules. He fought in the main battle at Agincourt where he was killed. His corpse was later identified by his shortened left arm, the result of an old wound.

Anthony, Duke of Brabant, arms quarterly 1&4 azure semee de lis or, a bordure compony gules and argent 2&3 sable a lion rampant or armed and langued gules. Younger brother of John the Fearless, Duke of Burgundy, he arrived late at the battle and, eager for glory, donned his trumpeter's banner as a coat of arms. Captured in the mêlée, he was unrecognized by his makeshift blazon and was killed in the massacre.

at-arms at least; this battle will be led by the Master of the Crossbowmen (+) and he will furnish up to this number from all the companies; this battle is to be held outside all the other battles to the left side, a little to the rear. And this battle is to strike the archers and do all in their power to break them. And when they set out to charge against the aforesaid archers, the foot battles and the wings are to march in order to advance together: and this battle will have half all the varlets of the company mounted on the best horses of their masters.

'Another battle will be made up to two hundred men-at-arms on horse together with the other half of all the varlets mounted on the best horses of their masters; and this battle will be led by Lord Bosredon; and this battle will strike to the rear of the English battle, against their varlets and their baggage and at the back of the English battle. And this battle will set out when the Master of Crossbows sets out to go and strike at the archers.'

Making allowances for the rather convoluted language, characteristic of the age, this is a brief but effective set of orders, giving us the who, the where and the how of the French plan. The dispositions are intended to mirror a typical English deployment and beat them at their own game. The mounted men give an extra dimension though and are intended to disrupt and neutralize their opponents' most fearsome weapon, the English archers. The use of varlets is interesting as it suggests that Boucicault and d'Albret were trying to make the most of their small force by deploying men not usually involved in the battle. Not that they were militarily useless, as the sergeants and *coustilliers* (so called after their long sword-like knife) could ride and use a sword effectively. In combat with lightly equipped archers, or coming by surprise upon the enemy rear, their lack of armour might be thought to be unimportant.

This then was the French plan: (1) to disrupt the English archery with a force under the Master of Crossbows appearing from behind the French line, advancing rapidly and smashing into enemy's the right flank; (2) at the same time to cause confusion by a rear attack; (3) to coordinate the cavalry attacks with an advance by the men on foot, the dismounted men-at-arms in the centre and the ordinary footmen on the flanks who would reply to English arrows with their own missiles, engage the English line without having taken heavy casualties from archery, and so win the day. As we shall see, French dispositions and tactics at Agincourt tried to employ just such an approach. Before moving on to this though, it is time to look at the English formation at Agincourt.

The English Battle Formation

It might seem surprising that there is anything new to say about this. It has been accepted for many years that Henry interspersed a line of dismounted men-at-arms with 'wedges' of archers. According to Lieutenant-Colonel Alfred Burne, writing during and after the Second World War, this was the formation at Crécy and one adopted by the English throughout the Hundred Years War. It was his interpretation of the meaning of the word 'herce', used by the chronicler Froissart to describe how the archers deployed for battle. Burne said that it meant 'harrow', an agricultural implement used to scour the earth before sowing. So he suggested that a 'herce' of archers meant a triangular formation, a wedge, projecting in front of the main battle line. He further went on to divide the English line into three divisions (the conventional three 'battles' of van, main body and rear), placing a wedge of archers on either side of these.

Unfortunately, this plan was entirely Burne's own invention. Jim Bradbury's recent book *The Medieval Archer* has studied the evidence carefully and concludes that archers were *never* interspersed in the main battle line. In fact, this would have weakened the formation considerably, for should heavily armoured knights have come up against unarmoured archers they could expect to disperse the bowmen quickly. Rather, Bradbury found that archers were always deployed to the flanks of the men-at-arms, although often inclining forward to direct a converging fire on an advancing enemy. This is the formation Henry used at Agincourt.

The situation has not been made easier by the Chaplain's assertion that the archers were formed up in 'wedges' in the English line. There are two problems here. One is that the Chaplain was

THE ENGLISH BATTLE FORMATION

certainly mistaken. He spent the entire battle with the baggage, a thousand yards behind the main line. Other accounts from men who actually took part in the battle describe the archers as on the wings. The second is that the Chaplain uses the word 'cuneus', or wedge, to describe the alleged formation, seemingly matching Burne's idea. 'Cuneus', however, does not just mean wedge but 'troop, body or unit' in a military sense. So this view can be discounted as misleading.

What then of the word 'herce'? (This term is not actually employed by any author to describe the archers at Agincourt.) Bradbury comes up with another derivation: that it could also mean like a 'hedge' or even 'spiky' like a hedgehog. This makes perfect sense, since the archers' stakes were truly spiky and would have presented the appearance of a hedge. I would like to refine this suggestion further. If we retain some of the meaning of 'harrow' and actually look at a picture of the implement, we can see that it forms a grid. If this pattern was used to deploy the archers, each behind a stake, it formed an excellent defensive position. Too many historians have assumed that the stakes were drawn up like the palings of a fence; but as John Keegan pointed out in *The Face of Battle*, this was too inflexible a barrier. Rather we should visualize a loose, checkerboard formation several ranks deep, allowing each man to see and shoot over the heads of those in front. This

still formed an impenetrable obstacle to horsemen but allowed the archers freedom of movement amongst a belt of stakes. This is what the Chaplain says:

'As a result of information divulged by some prisoners, a rumour went round the army that the enemy commanders had assigned certain bodies of

▲ *A harrow. Stakes arranged in this formation provided an impenetrable* *barrier against cavalry and protection for the lightly armoured English archers.*

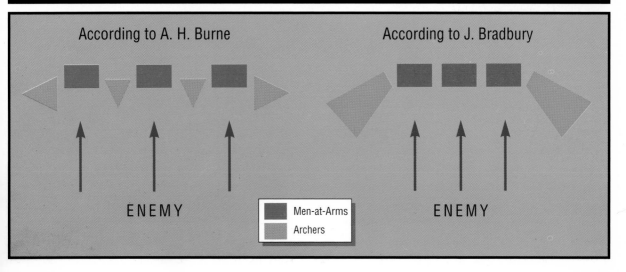

English Battle Formations Typical of the Period

According to A. H. Burne

According to J. Bradbury

ENEMY

ENEMY

Men-at-Arms

Archers

knights, many hundreds strong and mounted on barded horses, to break the formation and resistance of our archers when they engaged us in battle. The King, therefore, ordered that every archer, throughout the army, was to prepare and shape for himself a stake or staff, either square or round, but six feet long, of sufficient thickness and sharpened at both ends. And he commanded that whenever the French army approached to give battle and to break their ranks with such bodies of horsemen, all the archers were to drive their stakes in front of them in a line and some of them behind and in between the positions of the front rank, one end being driven into the ground pointing towards themselves, the other end pointing towards the enemy at above waist-height. So that the cavalry, when their charge had brought them close and in sight of the stakes, would either withdraw in great fear or, reckless of their own safety, run the risk of having both horses and riders impaled.'

The importance of intelligence about enemy intentions is highlighted by this. The French had not been aware of Henry's plan to get across the Somme, but he had information about their intended tactics. In this way the English had established the upper hand, although it probably did not seem that way on the morning of St Crispin's Day, 1415. St Rèmy states that 'many knowledgeable people' in the French army did not believe there would be any battle that day. They so obviously had the advantage, outnumbering the English by three or four to one in fighting men and

allowing no opportunity for Henry to slip away, that it seemed a humiliating negotiated settlement must be imposed upon him.

Negotiations and the Decision on Battle

Negotiations did take place after the opposing forces had been drawn up for battle. Some sources suggest that contact had already been made the previous night, since Henry was anxious to avoid a battle against such odds. St Rèmy states that the French demanded Henry give up his claim to the crown of France, together with newly captured Harfleur, while allowing him to retain Guienne. In response, Henry required the retention of Guienne, five named cities belonging to it, the

◀ *The battlefield, looking towards the English left (at the extreme edge of the Agincourt woods) from the French centre. The desperate nature of the boggy, ploughed land is evident from this shot taken in late October.*

▶ *Monumental brass of Sir John Drayton, about 1425, in Dorchester Abbey Church, Oxfordshire. Note the articulation of the upper arm defences.*

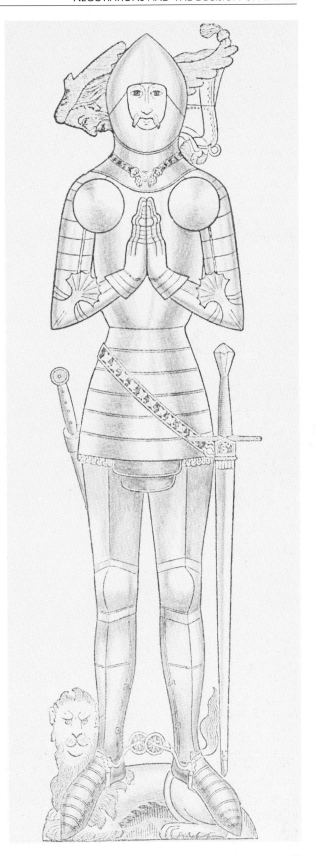

county of Ponthieu and marriage to King Charles's daughter, Katherine, with a dowry of 300,000 crowns! For this he was prepared to give up his claim and Harfleur. As all Henry's propaganda and efforts since he came to the throne had been directed to enforcing his claim to the French crown, despite the seeming boldness of the rest of his demands, this was still a climb-down. Just how serious were such negotiations must be open to doubt. While St Rèmy fancied that many in the French camp thought a battle unnecessary, Monstrelet, who was actually in it, says that the wiser heads saw it was the likely outcome.

Both sides had arrayed for battle at around eight o'clock. During the delay, the French sat around their standards breakfasting, laughing and forgiving each other their old quarrels. The English also took the opportunity to eat whatever meagre rations were available. Two or more hours passed. The French made no move, believing, quite correctly, that Henry had to drive them off in order to proceed to Calais, and that should he fail to do so he would fall into their hands. The English king took counsel from among his experienced lords. All agreed that there was nothing to be gained by waiting. The army was already weakened by disease and hunger, and, unlike the French who were in friendly territory, there was no chance of gathering supplies. The only option was attack, whatever the risk. Accordingly, Henry ordered his tiny force to advance against the enormous host opposing it.

Great care was taken to keep his men-at-arms and archers alike in formation, and to do it slowly so that they were not exhausted by moving over the sodden ground. When they came to within bow-shot of the enemy, perhaps a furlong (220 yards/ 200 metres) away, the English took up their positions.

The English Deployment

We have already looked at the English deployment in some detail. In the centre stood the 900 men-at-arms, around the standards of the King and the great nobles. Henry flew the banner of the Trinity, of St George, St Edward and his own arms. The Duke of Gloucester, Duke of York, Earl of March,

Earl of Huntingdon, the Earl of Oxford, the Earl of Kent, and the Lords of Roos and of Cornwall (those experienced knights who commanded the advance guard) also had their banners, together with many other lords. The King rode a small grey horse (its size distinguished it from a warhorse) and wore no spurs. This showed that he was going to dismount and fight on foot along with his men. First he rode along the lines making 'a fine address to them, exhorting them to act well; saying that he was come into France to recover his lawful inheritance, and that he had a good and just cause to claim it; that in that quarrel they might freely and surely fight; that they should remember they were born in the kingdom of England, where their mothers, wives and children now dwelt, and therefore they ought to strive to return there with great glory and fame; that the Kings of England, his predecessors, had gained many noble battles and successes over the French; that on that day everyone should endeavour to preserve his own person, and the honour of the crown of the King of England. He moreover reminded then that the French boasted that they would cut off three fingers from the right hand of every archer they might take, so that their shot should never again kill man or horse.' (St Rèmy)

The archers were deployed on the flanks of the small centre. It is not clear if they had planted their stakes at the start of the day. Deciding to advance, Henry moved his forces several hundred yards forward so that the English flanks rested on the woods around Agincourt and Tramecourt. In the new position some archers found themselves overlapping on to the outskirts of the woods, which also provided good protection. This may be the origin of the claim that Henry sent a special flanking force of 200 archers to Tramecourt in order to launch an ambush on the French. Monstrelet states that they slipped into a field near the French van and remained there, undiscovered, until the action began. It tells us a great deal about the spirit of the age that St Rèmy vigorously denies this 'accusation', as he sees it, stating that 'a man of honour who was that day in the company of the King of England, as I was, assured me the report was not true'. It seems likely that this manoeuvre, together with English mounted 'embuscades'

▶ *French crossbowman reloading, using a windlass. He wears a brigandine over mail and armour for his upper arm, but only a soft cap on his head. He would normally be paired with a pavise-bearer carrying a tall shield; but there is no reference to the latter at Agincourt, which would have made the French crossbowmen very vulnerable to English archery.*

claimed by some Frenchman did not in fact take place.

What then of the French, who had until now passively awaited the English approach?

The French Deployment

The French were drawn up in the conventional array of three battles: the van, centre and rear-guard. Constraints of space made it certain that these were one behind the other, although this may also have been the French commanders' intention. Contemporary assessment of their numbers range from 30,000 to 150,000. Certainly the force was very large. Chroniclers who were present at the battle speak of it being from three to six times as big as the English. It is normally dangerous to take medieval writers at their word, but the 20-30,000 men such a calculation gives is not unreasonable. There were many named lords present, each of whom had followings, so that Burne's estimate of 25,000 looks to be about right.

Monstrelet, who fought in the battle, gives the most detailed account. He says that the first division contained 8,000 'bascinets' (meaning men-at-arms), 4,000 archers and 1,500 cross-bowmen. This was commanded by the Constable, who was accompanied by the Dukes of Orleans and Bourbon, the Counts of Eu and Richemont, Marshal Boucicault, the Lord of Dampierre, Admiral of France, and Guichard Dauphin. The Master of Crossbows, David de Rambures, was also in the van, although the original plan assigned him the outflanking force. His mounted command was now given to the Count of Vendôme, who was assigned 1,600 men on the left flank. On the right Clignet de Brébant was assigned 800 mounted men-at-arms, all picked men. Other leaders who featured in these vital forces were the Saveuse brothers, William (of whom we shall hear later), Hector and Philip, Ferry de Mailly, Aliaume de Gapaines, Allain de Vendonne, Lanion de Launay and others. The flanking forces of cavalry seem to have been drawn up in line with, or slightly in advance of, the first battle.

Behind this stood the second division, of a similar size or slightly smaller. It consisted of some 3-6,000 men-at-arms and 'gros valets' (the armed servant and second man in each lance) under the command of the Dukes of Bar and Alençon, the Counts of Nevers, de Vaudemont, de Blaumont, de Salines, de Grand-pré and de Roussy. Some accounts place the French missile-men in the second battle. Historians have suggested that they were bundled out of their proper position by their social superiors, the nobles and knights eager for glory in what they anticipated as an easy victory. Certainly the French archers and crossbowmen, who had an important role in the original plan, that of countering English archery, seem to have taken little or no part. The French chronicler Des Ursins asserts that they did not loose an arrow or a bolt in the whole encounter.

The third division was made up of mounted men-at-arms, supposedly, 8-10,000 strong if we can rely on the previous figures. In addition there were at least as many non-combatants as fighting men. The proportion might even have been two to

▶ *The dense woods surrounding Tramecourt, on the French left. This obstacle prevented the French from deploying their superior numbers.*

one. (To create a visual image of the discrepancy in numbers between the two sides, one only has to imagine the difference between a sparsely attended English Fourth Division football game and Anfield full to bursting, with the Kop in full cry.)

Phase 1: The English Advance and the French Cavalry Charges

After the period of waiting, as we have seen, Henry decided to advance. The armies were some 1,000 yards apart. The English advanced slowly, keeping good order and with many pauses for breath. The ground was sodden with the autumn rain and planted with young wheat, producing a slippery and glutinous mess underfoot that must have been especially tiring for the men in armour. They seem to have moved up to within 250-300 yards of the enemy, extreme effective arrow range, where they took up the positions previously described. The archers must have taken their stakes with them, for Waurin describes them 'making a hedge in front of them with which they fortified themselves'.

Once in this position the archers began to shoot at the enemy. Just imagine for a moment that you are an archer in the English army. You are famished, cold and wet and suffering from diarrhoea or worse from the effects of your diet of unclean water and nuts and berries. You expect to die in the forthcoming battle. For the men-at-arms there will be ransoms and often cosy captivity at the hands of men of their own class, related by birth or known to them personally. As a despised and feared footman, all you can expect is to be slaughtered by men so well-armoured as to be almost invulnerable, or, if captured, to be mutilated so that you may not ply your craft again. The King has just reminded you that you can expect to lose three fingers from your right hand. However rousing his speech, you are most fortified by

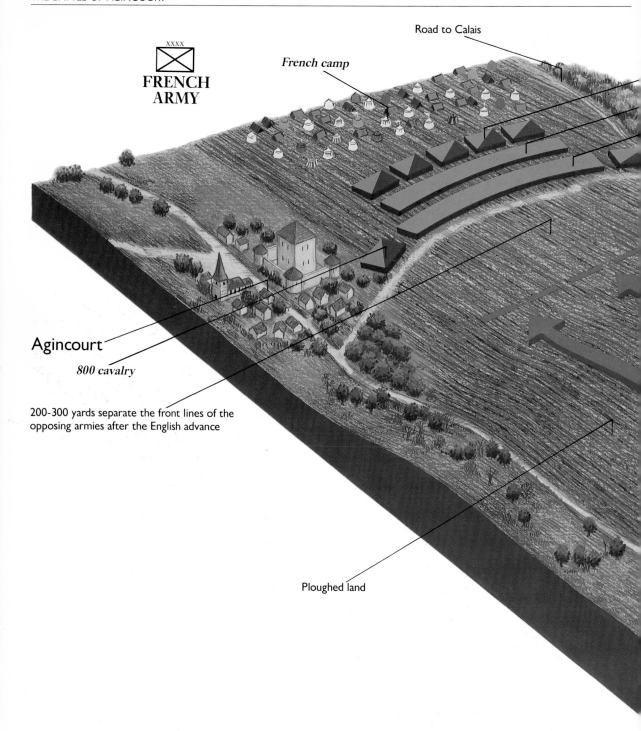

Road to Calais

French camp

XXXX
FRENCH
ARMY

Agincourt

800 cavalry

200-300 yards separate the front lines of the
opposing armies after the English advance

Ploughed land

THE BATTLE OF AGINCOURT

**Initial positions, about 1100 hours, 25 October 1415; as seen
from the south.**

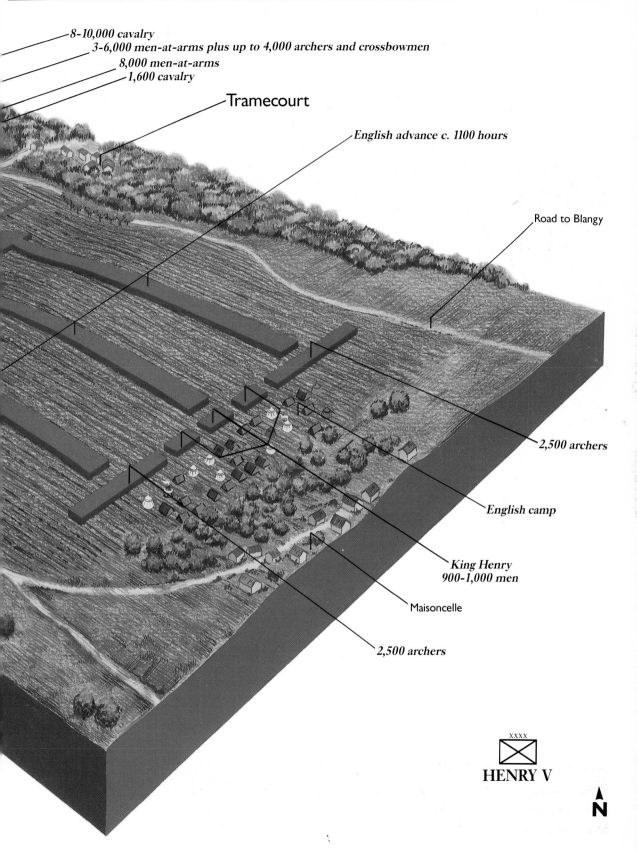

8-10,000 cavalry

3-6,000 men-at-arms plus up to 4,000 archers and crossbowmen

8,000 men-at-arms

1,600 cavalry

Tramecourt

English advance c. 1100 hours

Road to Blangy

2,500 archers

English camp

King Henry
900-1,000 men

Maisoncelle

2,500 archers

XXXX
HENRY V

N

despair. At first it seems impossible that the French can be beaten. Then as you advance it becomes apparent that they have been careless – that they do not know what they are doing!

The English archery seems to have stirred the French to action. First their crossbowmen loosed off a hasty volley, then fell back for fear of the English arrows. Then their two wings of cavalry launched a charge across the intervening ground. Things went wrong from the very first. To begin with: organization. The horsemen were supposed to be 1,600 and 800 strong on the left and right flanks respectively. But the French sources lament that such numbers were never collected. One (the Berry Herald) asserts that many knights from throughout the host had wandered off, out of their positions during the long period of waiting. Monstrelet says that the right wing, led with some panache by William of Saveuse, mustered barely 150 men (seven score). St Rèmy, on the other side, assigns him 300 lances and Clignet de Brébant a mere 160 (eight score). Evidently the flank charges were seriously undermanned. Further, they could not really be described as flank charges. In the original plan these forces had been designed to strike at the flank and rear of the English. At Agincourt this proved impossible, since the English flanks rested on woods. St Rèmy actually says that the attacks were designed to go 'by' Agincourt and Tramecourt, though whether this implies a deliberate flanking attack is difficult to say. Certainly there was an attack on the English camp, as

we shall see later, although the sources are unclear as to whether this was intended to act in concert with the flank charges.

In the event, the two attacks were not pressed with much vigour. It is doubtful whether the French cavalry could have got up much speed over recently ploughed, rain-soaked ground. Just how slippery the surface was can be gathered from St Rèmy's account of William of Saveuse's charge. He is described as a valiant knight who encouraged his men to throw their mounts upon the archers' stakes. The ground was so soft that the stakes fell down, enabling the force to withdraw with the loss of only three men. But clearly not all the stakes fell down or the French would have broken through and ridden down the archers. The sort of thicket

◄ The battlefield, looking from the English right-centre some 400 yards from the probable position of the French first line just beyond the white houses.

hedge that has been described nullified the impetus of an already laboured charge. Having performed their duty, the horsemen duly made off. What of the three men who died? They shared the fate of their leader, William de Saveuse, whose horse collided with a stake that held firm. As a result he was propelled over his mount's head to lie stunned and helpless at the feet of the English archers, by whom he was swiftly dispatched. The loss of their dashing commander must have taken the heart out of the French. The English bowmen began to shoot at their now-retreating enemy, maddening the horses with arrow wounds. A similar drama was acted out on the other side of the battlefield.

Where were the panicking men and their by now uncontrollable mounts to go? On an open battlefield they could have filtered around the flanks of their own forces. Some had in fact been driven into the woods on either side of the battlefield. The rest propelled themselves violently into the by now advancing first division of the French army. One chronicler, the Richemont Herald, who served the Duke of Richemont, a participant at the battle, puts the blame on these horsemen for the entire defeat. It was because they were a bunch of cowardly Lombards and Gascons, he avers, that they performed as they did. The Herald's prejudice is unwarranted, but his analysis is accurate and shared by every other writer present at, or reporting, the battle. As the defeated horsemen streamed back, they burst into the French formation, causing it to fall into almost total disarray. John Keegan's image of a panicking police horse in a crowd, producing a sort of 'ripple effect', as people were knocked against one-another, is a telling one. This disruption was repeated hundreds of times over and magnified by its repetition.

Phase 2: The Main French Attack and Mêlée

Now, instead of being a menacing and over-whelming powerful force, the French first battle, full of the cream of their army, was vulnerable and already half-beaten. The Chaplain claims that they were able to reorganize sufficiently to form them-selves into three bodies, with which they assaulted

THE BATTLE OF AGINCOURT

as seen from the north; about 1200–1400 hours, 25 October 1415.

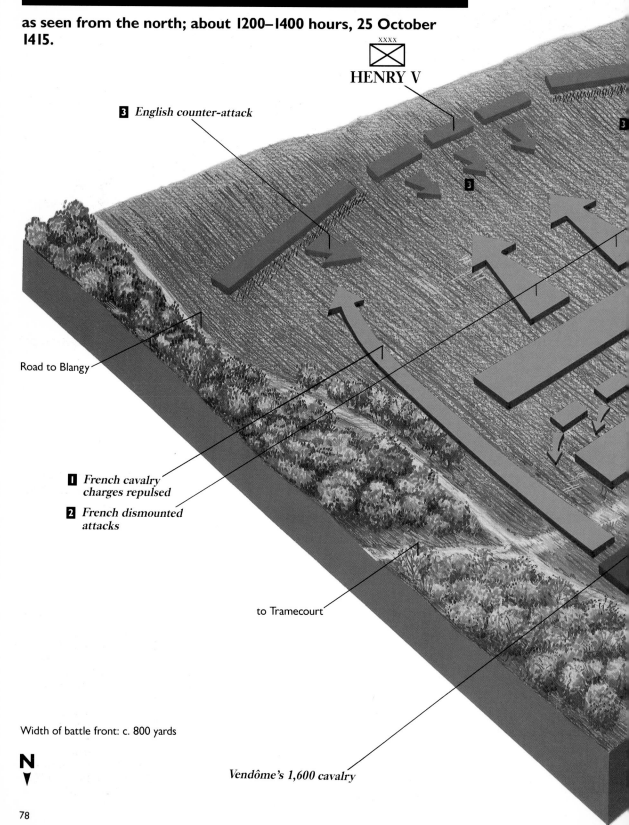

XXXX

HENRY V

3 *English counter-attack*

Road to Blangy

1 *French cavalry charges repulsed*

2 *French dismounted attacks*

to Tramecourt

Width of battle front: c. 800 yards

N

Vendôme's 1,600 cavalry

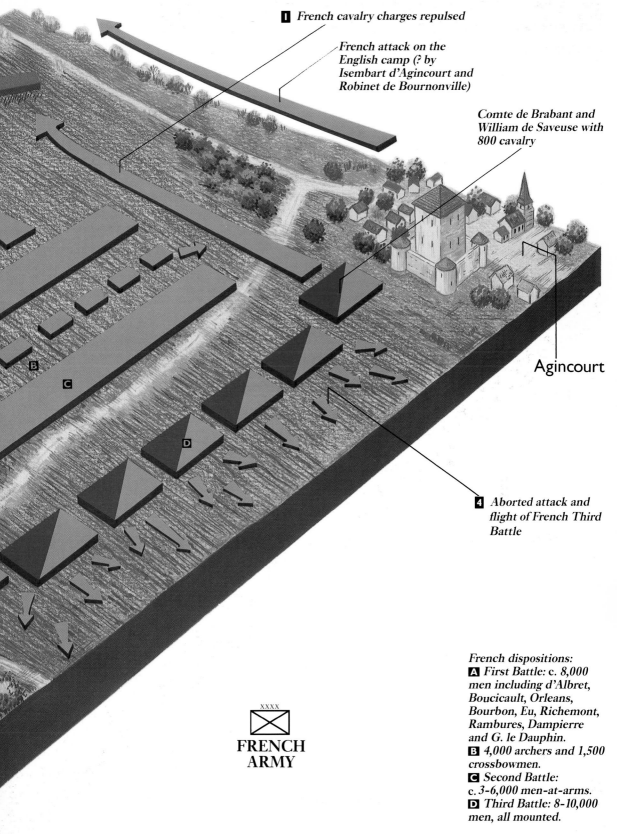

1 *French cavalry charges repulsed*

*French attack on the
English camp (? by
Isembart d'Agincourt and
Robinet de Bournonville)*

*Comte de Brabant and
William de Saveuse with
800 cavalry*

Agincourt

4 *Aborted attack and
flight of French Third
Battle*

xxxx

**FRENCH
ARMY**

French dispositions:
A *First Battle: c. 8,000
men including d'Albret,
Boucicault, Orleans,
Bourbon, Eu, Richemont,
Rambures, Dampierre
and G. le Dauphin.*
B *4,000 archers and 1,500
crossbowmen.*
C *Second Battle:
c. 3-6,000 men-at-arms.*
D *Third Battle: 8-10,000
men, all mounted.*

the standards. That is to say, the three positions in the English line where the commanders of the three divisions, van, centre and rear, stood. This may have been possible, and Keegan envisages the archers funnelling the French armoured knights towards their own men-at-arms. This supposes that the English stood in three separate divisions, each flanked by archers, which is no longer tenable. Better perhaps to listen to contemporaries who tell us that the French fell into complete disarray after intermingling with the defeated cavalry. They pressed on though. Honour demanded that they cross swords with the men-at-arms opposing them. In fact, they carried lances, shortened to some five or six feet to make them less prone to breaking and more manageable on foot. But they were already near exhaustion. The ground they were crossing, unlike that traversed by the English earlier in the day, was a morass. It had been broken up by the horses of their army, which had been exercised by the pages and varlets throughout the cold night; it had been further churned up by the cavalry charge and its returning horses; now thousands of heavily-armoured men, perhaps eight to ten ranks deep, ploughed it still further.

The arrow storm forced every man to keep his head down for fear that a shaft might penetrate the eye slits in his helmet. Furthermore the English stood with the low, winter sun behind them – another unnerving and disorientating factor. As the range shortened, there can be no doubt that English bodkin arrows, designed for the job, began to go through even plate armour protection. When the French arrived at the English line, after three hundred yards of blind, muscle-wrenching foot-slogging, there can have been no impetus left. Perhaps they did push the English back a few yards, represented poetically as a 'lance's length'. But many of the French must have been stupefied with exhaustion. And they were so crowded together that even if they had the strength to lift their weapons there was no space in which to aim a blow.

The fighting was nevertheless intense. The English did suffer casualties, the most notable of whom was the Duke of York. He probably was not suffocated under a mound of bodies as is usually claimed, but had his helmet beaten in so that it smashed his skull. The same fate nearly befell the King. All the eighteen squires who had supposedly sworn to fell Henry were killed, but somebody (perhaps one of them or possibly the Duke of Alençon) struck him a blow on the helmet which lopped a fleuret off the gold crown and left it heavily dented. Henry was certainly in the thick of the action. He stood over the badly wounded Earl of Oxford and prevented him from being killed by the French. The battle between the men-at-arms seems to have been very close fought. Surprisingly, perhaps, the most effective intervention in the outcome of the fighting seems to have been provided by the lightly-equipped archers. All accounts describe them as throwing down their bows and engaging in the fray. They were equipped with swords, including the chopping falchion, axes and heavy mallets (used for hammering in the stakes and now for beating down the enemy). Their nimbleness, being so lightly clad upon the heavy ground, made them more than a match for the exhausted and bemused men-at-arms who opposed them – men, furthermore, who despised the low-born archers but now fell easy prey to them.

So the seemingly impossible happened. The small English force began to drive the French in front of it, killing, beating down and taking prisoner all who opposed them. Some chronicles speak of piles of dead as high as a man. While there were doubtless many bodies strewn around, some dead, some unconscious, some merely trapped, such a thing is a physical impossibility; but it captures the feeling of a massacre. The first French division was now forced back on to the second. But this strengthening of the French line seems to have had no effect. It merely produced the same results as before. On all sides French men-at-arms, including the most nobly-born amongst them, were giving themselves up. This was a risky business in the heat of battle. Too many Frenchmen seem to have seen the mêlée as a sort

▶Henry V and the Duke d'Alençon at Agincourt. A romantic Edwardian depiction from the picture by Arthur Twidle.

of joust between gentlemen, in which it was possible to hand over one's glove as a symbol of surrender when a duel had been concluded with honour on both sides. The Duke of Alençon lost his life in this way, as doubtless did many others. We are told that after sparring with Henry but finding himself worsted he attempted to give himself up. As he did so, he was struck down by a battle-crazed Englishman, and so died.

The third division, looking on with horror at the defeat of the first two, made no move. Some indeed, being mounted, rode off in flight. Some of the luckier men-at-arms among the first two battles were also helped to their horses by their retainers and so escaped. But all the leaders of the French were killed or fell into English hands.

Both the instigators of the French battle plan, the Constable and the Marshal, were lost: d'Albret was killed and Boucicault captured. We have already seen how many of those named in the plan suffered one or the other fate. With all its chief leaders gone, the French host, although still formidable, was quite impotent – or was it? There was another act in the drama yet to come, one that has produced great feelings of horror and repugnance from many (mainly French) historians.

Phase 3: The Killing of the Prisoners

The battle itself had been very brief. It may have only taken half-an-hour, although some accounts give two three hours (which probably included some of the preliminaries). It was now early afternoon on a short, late October day. The English were looking to gather their prisoners and tot-up the lucrative ransoms they had made, as well as tending to their wounds and catching their breath. The battle was apparently over, the French utterly defeated and in flight. But something happened to cause Henry to order an action that quite offended against the conventions of warfare: the slaughter of a large part of those taken prisoner. In fact, two things happened.

The first was the report brought to Henry that his camp was being attacked. Exactly when or how this was carried out is far from clear. The conventional story accepted by chroniclers after the battle was that the local lord, Isembart

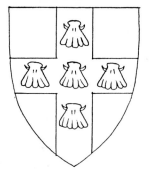

▲*Waleran, Count of Fauquembergues, arms or on a cross sable five escallops argent.*

▶ *Waleran de Raineval, Count de Fauquembergues, leading the third division in the final fruitless charge at Agincourt. Unlike the dismounted knights, he has retained his shield and lance and has his visor closed against the arrow-storm. His horse wears protection for head, neck and chest and a caparison decorated with the count's arms.*

d'Agincourt, assisted by Robinet de Bournonville, Riflart de Clamasse and several other men-at-arms, leading 600 peasants, of their own volition launched a raid on the camp. Certainly several precious items, a crown, some silver and a precious sword were looted from the camp. It was later a condition of the ransom of Ralph de Gaucourt that he recover these items. He was successful in part. The story also goes that d'Agincourt and Bournonville were afterwards imprisoned by the Duke of Burgundy for this disgraceful act, despite their making a present of the sword to his son. But all this may be no more than an after-the-event justification to blame somebody for the ensuing tragedy.

The second action that spurred the massacre was the attempted counter-attack by a remnant of the third division. Amid all the confusion, several lords, named as the Counts of Marle and Fauquembergh and the Lords of Louvroy and Chin, managed to gather together six hundred men-at-arms. With them they made a mounted charge, which, according to Monstrelet, ended as disastrously as all the others. To the Chaplain it seemed as if this was the moment that Henry ordered the prisoners to be killed. To Monstrelet, as we have seen, the cause was the unsanctioned rear attack. Both actions were used to blame their participants for the carnage that followed. Both, had they turned the course of the battle, would have doubtless been recorded as strokes of brilliance.

The English, although victorious, were very vulnerable. They had by no means secured all their prisoners or accepted their surrender. There were still more than enough heavily armed Frenchmen at liberty to overwhelm the English should they recover their morale. So Henry gave the order to kill the prisoners. Only the most prominent were to be spared, such as the Dukes of Orleans and Bourbon. But, as we have seen, high birth was no guarantee at such a moment. The knights and men-at-arms considered it an ignoble act and beneath their dignity to engage in killing defenceless men, so the task was carried out by a squire commanding two hundred archers. Even compared with the mayhem of battle it must have been a grim sight. How were the French killed? St

Rèmy, who witnessed the massacre, describes them as 'cut in pieces, heads and faces'. Indeed that was the only place where a knight in full armour was truly vulnerable. Only if they removed a man's helmet or lifted his visor could he be killed easily. Those who resisted even this would have been stabbed through the eye-slit in their bascinet. Such cold-blooded killing appalled contemporaries, not so much for how it was done, although that did matter, but for whom it was done to. The men killed were noblemen and gentlemen, not the low-born who were expected to die in a battle. The men who wrote the accounts came from these upper classes, and such brutal realities clashed with the image of war as a gentlemanly pursuit, which they generally promulgated. But, as we have seen, they did not blame Henry for carrying out this brutal necessity, but rather those leaders who so alarmed him as to bring the situation about.

The French Plan Revisited

So far the description of the rear attack at Agincourt has been taken at face value from the contemporary chroniclers: that it was an extemporised attack by a greedy local lord. But it also fits well into the original French plan. This had envisaged an attack sweeping around on to the left rear of the English army, in conjunction with the cavalry charge on to its right flank. We do not know when the attack on the camp took place. Some accounts suggest that it happened early in the battle; others link it with the counter-attack from a part of the mounted third division. If it had been designed to coincide with frontal assaults, then it reproduced the French tactics in full. After all, who better to lead such an assault than the local lord who knew his way through the woods? Remember too that, on the evening before, Henry was alarmed by the thought of just such a flank attack delivered behind cover of the trees on either side of the eventual battlefield.

If this interpretation is accepted, and it is the one proposed by Chris Philpotts, the young scholar who found the manuscript containing the plan, then we must credit the French at Agincourt with a great deal more sense than has previously been thought possible. This is true in part, at least. For contemporaries are quite right in blaming the French for the carelessness that comes from over-confidence. The very same men who made the battle plan that could have defeated the English proved incapable of putting it into effect. The fault here lay once more with the lack of a single leader in the French camp.

Experienced and important though they were, the Constable and Marshal, as the King's officers, could not outrank Princes of the Blood. Operating on their own with a small command and amenable companions, they might have got the plan to work. But once they were lumbered with a huge force and all the competing jealousies and arrogance of the French higher nobility, they had no chance. D'Albret and Boucicault were in the front rank of the van along with all the nobles whose ambition for military glory they admittedly shared. Meanwhile lax discipline allowed men to wander out of the ranks and led to the crucial undermanning of the two cavalry wings; Furthermore, since everyone could see (with hindsight) that the battlefield was too narrow for the number of men with them, could they not have redeployed elsewhere?

Once again the problem was one of a cumbersome force that could scarcely be manoeuvred. But also the army had been raised to combat the King's enemies in a trial by battle on ground that had been selected by the French commanders out of several possible sites. There could be no retreat from such a position. As a result of a combination of tactical and mental inflexibility, the English won the day. And they won by displaying virtues that were the reverse of the French coin: dogged resilience and initiative in the face of danger, provided in large part by the genius of their commander.

After the last trace of any French threat had ended, leaving Henry the master of the field and all the enemy's food and equipment, he withdrew once more to camp at Maisoncelle. The following day he resumed the march to Calais.

▶ *Brass of Sir John Lysle in Thruxton Church, Hampshire. He died in 1407, but the brass was not laid until some thirteen years later, so that it shows armour typical of the end of Henry V's reign, all plate and here with ornamental elbow-pieces.*

THE OUTCOME OF THE BATTLE

Henry did not, and could not, move to the immediate exploitation of his victory. He took his exhausted and bedraggled army, together with its magnificent haul of prisoners, on a slow, three-day march to Calais. Here he remained for a fortnight, arranging the crossing and awaiting a favourable wind. He landed at Dover on 16 November, and a week later was greeted at London with an elaborate and lavish pageant. A victory song repeated the refrain: 'Deo gratias Anglia redde pro victoria' – it was by God's will that Henry and the English had triumphed. Henry had justified his claim to be called 'King of England and of France'.

Why then had he not marched straight to Paris to enforce his claim? Simply, it was late in the campaigning season and his army was battered and out of supplies. True, the French had suffered a disastrous defeat, but cities did not fall to a few thousand men without siege equipment. In fact, it took another five years to bring Charles VI to the Treaty of Troyes, by which Henry married his daughter Katherine and was recognized as the heir to the French throne. Territory was not won by open battle, but by long sieges, such as those of Caen and Rouen. Agincourt aside, the main result of the 1415 campaign was the capture of Harfleur as another base from which to attack Normandy, the necessary foundation for a long-term strategy of conquest. The town was besieged by the French in the following year, but they were driven off largely as a result of an English naval victory below its walls.

▼ *The clump of trees surrounds the Calvary, a monument erected to the French dead in the last century. It marks the site of some of the extensive grave pits and is a hundred yards from the small road linking Agincourt and Tramecourt. French men-at-arms would have been easy targets for archery at this range.*

Northern France to 1422

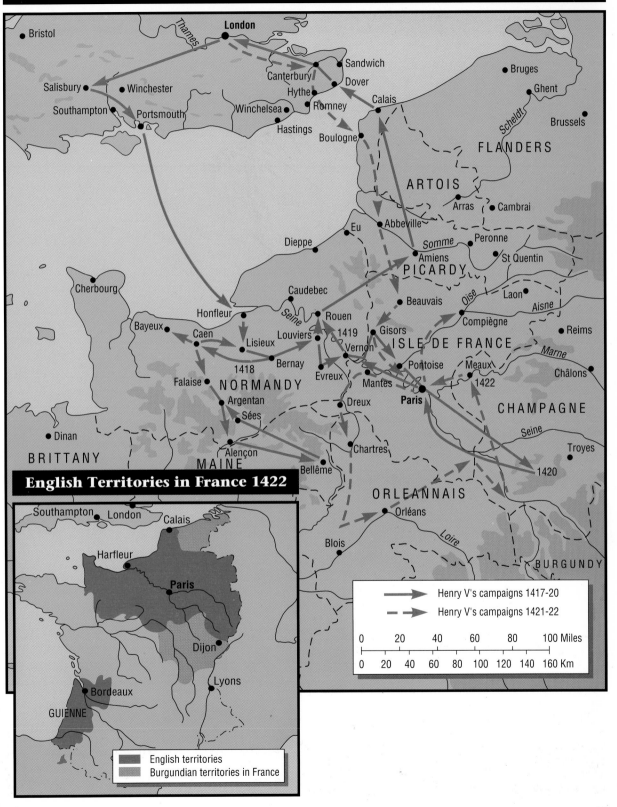

English Territories in France 1422

Henry V's campaigns 1417-20
Henry V's campaigns 1421-22

| 0 | 20 | 40 | 60 | 80 | 100 Miles |

| 0 | 20 | 40 | 60 | 80 | 100 | 120 | 140 | 160 Km |

English territories
Burgundian territories in France

▲ *The Calvary, surrounded by its clump of trees, is an important landmark for reconstructing the battle, as it probably stands in the centre of the French position.*

Yet Agincourt was a grievous blow to French morale and to Charles VI's capacity to resist. First, the outcome suggested to everyone that justice lay with the English. One chronicler ascribed the defeat to divine revenge. For the battle fell on the feast day of Saints Crispin and Crispianus, closely associated with the city of Soissons, sacked by the Armagnac faction a year earlier. The physical loss was immense too. Some 600 members of the baronage and knightly class fell at Agincourt. Five dukes, twelve counts and numerous other social and political leaders were in captivity. A French historian, Françoise Autrand, has calculated that one third of King Charles's 1,400-strong political supporters were swept away by the catastrophe.

They all came from the northern provinces where the King recruited his military and civil servants. This 'decapitation' of the royal military structure and disorganization of its economic resources seriously reduced the French Crown's capacity to resist English aggression. So, in that respect, it made Henry's eventual victory the easier to achieve.

Ironically, the young King was to predecease his elderly father-in-law by seven weeks. He was never to hold the dual monarchy, which fell instead to his infant son. The Hundred Years War was not over, but Henry V had initiated a period of English supremacy that was to endure for a generation.

◀ *The ceramic model at the battlefield today, showing the campaign (right) and battle (left). Note especially the suggested boundaries of the woods. The square block on the left of the English line represents Agincourt castle.*

THE BATTLEFIELD TODAY

The village of Azincourt lies just off the D928 some 45 miles (75km) south-east of Calais. There is a museum in the village hall in the centre, opposite the church. This contains an audio-visual display evoking the battle, reconstructed arms and armour, and a few floor tiles from the long-gone castle. It also provides leaflets in English and French, a poster and other literature. A three-mile battlefield walk takes the visitor through the main battle area, via a Calvary near the grave pits and a monument with a battle map, through Maisoncelle and back to Azincourt.

▶ Agincourt church. The monument to the left of the crucifix bears the portraits of four village men killed in the much greater conflict of the First World War. On the opposite side of the square is the small but interesting visitor centre, which has a slide-and-tape display about the battle. The key is held at the Mairie nearby.

CHRONOLOGY

1392 Charles VI's first attack of insanity.
1399 Henry IV usurps throne; young Henry becomes Prince of Wales.
1403 Battle of Shrewsbury.
1404 John the Fearless becomes Duke of Burgundy.
1405 English land in the Côtentin Peninsula; French land in Wales.
1407 Assassination of Louis, Duke of Orleans.
1409 Peace of Chartres between French princes.
1410 English attack on Fécamp.
1411–13 Conflicts and disorder in Paris.
1413 Henry V becomes King of England.
1414–15 Embassies exchanged between England and France.

1415 English invasion of Normandy:
11 August English fleet sails from Southampton.
14 August English disembark near Harfleur.
18 August Harfleur completely surrounded.
3 September Dauphin Louis takes French force to Vernon on borders of Normandy.
10 September Charles VI raises the war-standard at St Denis.
14 September (approx.) Constable d'Albret to Honfleur; Marshal Boucicault to Caudebec.
15 September French sally burns siege castle opposite Leure Gate.
16 September Main bastion captured by the English; French agree to surrender if no relief comes within a week.
23 September English enter the town.
27 September Henry offers personal combat to the Dauphin Louis.
8 October English set out from Harfleur for Calais; French covering forces march to River Somme.
9 October English near Fécamp.
11 October English encounter resistance at Arques.

12 October English reach Eu.
13 October Henry discovers the Somme is blocked at the ford of Blanchetacque.
14 October English at Hangest.
15 October English arrive opposite Amiens and spend night at Pont de Metz; main French force sets out from Rouen.
16 October English spend night at Boves.
17 October Skirmish at Corbie; Henry force-marches south.
18 October English arrive near Nesle; French main body arrives at Amiens.
19 October Henry slips his force over the Somme at Voyennes and Bethencourt fords.
20 October Henry rests his exhausted army.
21 October English advance to near Albert.
22 October English reach Forceville, shadowed by the united French force to their right.
23 October English cross the River Ternoise at Blangy.
24 October French block the English route to Calais at Agincourt-Tramecourt; English spend the night at Maisoncelle.
25 October Battle of Agincourt.
28 October English arrive at Calais.
23 November Victory parade in London.

1416 English naval victory off Harfleur.
1417 English besiege and capture Caen.
1419 English besiege and capture Rouen, securing Normandy; assassination of John the Fearless; Anglo-Burgundian alliance.
1420 Treaty of Troyes: Henry V marries Katherine of France and becomes heir to the French throne.
1421 French victory at Baugé; Thomas, Duke of Clarence, killed.
1422 Siege and capture of Meaux; Henry V falls ill and dies; Charles VI dies; Henry's one-year-old son becomes King of England and France.

A GUIDE TO FURTHER READING

BRADBURY, J. *The Medieval Archer*, Woodbridge, 1985. Excellent history of archery tactics.

BURNE, A. H. *The Agincourt War*, London, 1956. Dated and quirky, but some useful insights.

CONTAMINE, P., trans. M. Jones. *War in the Middle Ages*, Oxford, 1984. A general survey, but detailed and scholarly with an excellent bibliography.

HARRISS, G. L., ed. *Henry V: the practise of Kingship*, Oxford, 1985. Collection of articles; see especially C. T. Allmand on Henry as a soldier.

FOWLER, K. *The Age of Plantagenet and Valois*, London, 1980. Lavishly illustrated, but scholarly, thematic survey of the Hundred Years, War.

JACOB, E. F. *Henry V and the Invasion of France*, London, 1947. Old but very accomplished study.

KEEGAN, J. *The Face of Battle*, London, 1976. Fascinating analysis of the realities of war.

NICOLAS, Sir H. *History of the Battle of Agincourt*, London, 2nd ed. 1832, repr. London 1970. An invaluable collection of translated documents and chronicles.

PHILPOTTS, C. 'The French plan of battle during the Agincourt campaign' in *English Historical Review*, pp.59-68, London, 1984.

TAYLOR, F. and ROSKELL, R. S. trans/ed. *Gesta Henrici Quinti (The Deeds of Henry the Fifth)* Oxford, 1975. Excellent modern edition of the 'Chaplain's' account.

SEWARD, D. *Henry V as Warlord*, London, 1987. General biography with emphasis on military affairs.

WARGAMING AGINCOURT

Wargames that seek to recreate historical events are not unlike theatrical performances: both attempt to suspend disbelief, to involve participants in a visual spectacle and an emotional or intellectual conflict and – of course! – to entertain. The game designer or organizer is the director; the players are the stars who will take the leading roles; and the miniature lead or plastic troops are the non-speaking parts or 'extras'. It seems appropriate, therefore, since the popular view of Agincourt is largely derived from Shakespeare's *Henry V*, to present the wargame as a play in four acts, whose several scenes will portray the different aspects of the campaign.

Act I: 'Once More Unto the Breach' The Siege of Harfleur

The progress of the siege falls into three separate, distinct types of scene: the initial blockade and bombardment or mining of the walls to create a practicable breach, which may be interrupted by sorties by the garrison to destroy the besiegers' works and engines; the storming of the outworks (and, should the garrison refuse to surrender, of the town itself); and the summons to surrender and negotiations between the representatives of the besieging forces and those of the garrison and/or inhabitants of the town. Players will take the roles of Henry V, his master engineer, responsible for construction and siting of siege engines, mines and bombards, and Lord de Gaucourt, the commander of the Harfleur garrison, while other roles may be created on either side to occupy additional participants. An umpire will be responsible for recording their actions, the consumption of supplies, the outbreak of disease in the besiegers' camp or starvation in the town, and will resolve the effects of bombardment, mining and counter-mining.

The French players and the umpire should have a detailed, scale plan of the town and its immediate surroundings. The English players, however, must draw their own map from perspective views of Harfleur, drawn as if from various vantage points around the town, presented to them by the umpire. King Henry's master engineer must then advise his sovereign on the town's weak points and the correct siting of mines, engines or bombards. If sufficient players are available, several rival engineers may present opposing theories in a short committee game, dominated by technical discussion, victory going to the engineer entrusted with the control of the siege by the King – though the subsequent progress of the siege may show this trust to have been misplaced! Engineers' briefings will need to contain plenty of abstruse Latin terms and arcane theories to baffle the simple soldiers: works such as Contamine's *War in the Middle Ages* will provide inspiration.

Once the English have positioned their engines and planned the routes of their mines on their sketch map, the umpire can transfer the information to his scale plan to determine their effectiveness. In the early stages of the siege, each game turn might represent a week; later the tension may be heightened by adopting daily turns, as the walls crumble and mines creep towards their targets. The umpire can determine the damage caused by bombardment by simple mathematical calculations, based upon the number and weight of projectiles and the strength of that part of the wall, informing the French of the exact damage but telling the English only what they would perceive from their siege lines. Thus, for example, only the garrison would be aware of deaths caused by random stone projectiles landing on buildings inside the town walls, the exact nature of the damage caused to the fortifications and the time or number of labourers required to effect repairs.

Tunnels dug by both besieger and besieged will be plotted on transparent sheets, which the umpire can overlay on his master map to determine whether the miners are close enough to detect each other's presence, and when tunnels are intercepted. The resulting subterranean conflicts may be resolved by a simple die roll, chance cards, or fought out with model figures on a plan of the tunnels. Players, taking the roles of individual miners, would each have an individual display, representing what they could see or feel in the dark, and inform the umpire of their actions in secret. The umpire would determine which players had come into contact, and place appropriate figures on their personal displays. Combat would be resolved quickly and brutally: both players would simultaneously present cards from a selection listing various blows, thrusts or parries (or even panic-stricken flight!) comparison of which would determine the victor and the infliction of wounds or death.

Space precludes a more detailed explanation of this game structure, but those who wish to try it will find a full description in my article 'Wargaming Night Actions' in *Miniature Wargames*, number 15, page 17.

The besiegers will have no difficulty foraging for food in the countryside around Harfleur, but as the siege continues they will run an increasing risk that disease will break out in their insanitary camps. The umpire will dice to discover whether disease afflicts the English army and the number of deaths each day; English players will draw chance cards to discover whether their characters fall sick and, if so, for how long they are incapacitated. Chance cards or dice will also be used to introduce random events, such as the bursting of guns or the flooding or collapse of mines.

The garrison will, once the town has been invested, have to husband its supplies of food carefully if it is to withstand a long siege. At the start of the game the umpire will inform the garrison commander how many days' food is in store for his troops. De Gaucourt must decide whether to expel the civilian population in order to save food, thereby losing a source of labour with which to repair damage to the walls and incurring considerable unpopularity, or to reduce the rations, risking an increased likelihood of disease and reducing the effectiveness of his troops in combat.

The French may make sorties in an attempt to destroy the besiegers' works, or simply to delay the inexorable progress of the siege in the hope that relief arrives in time. These sorties may be resolved by dice and their effect upon the siege calculated by the umpire, or fought as small skirmishes using the system for gaming hand-to-hand combat described below, or as conventional wargames with figures.

Outworks or the town itself – if negotiations fail – may have to be stormed. Players will take the roles of individual men-at-arms on each side, and move their personal figures, accompanied by others representing their retinues, sundry varlets and peasant scum, on a model of the breach, ideally in the same scale as the figures, strewn with expanded polystyrene 'rubble', balsa wood or matchstick planks and other debris. Movement over the breach will be determined by die rolls, to reflect the troops' difficulty in clambering over the rubble, and casualties. Players who throw a 1 are assumed to have fallen over and will have to throw more than 1, or 2 if armoured, in order to regain their feet in a subsequent turn. The umpire will throw dice to discover if anyone is hit by random arrows or other projectiles: armoured warriors will have a greater chance of surviving unwounded but may be knocked down and temporarily stunned by a blow. Personal combat will be resolved using the adaptation of the 'Chivalry' system described in the final Act, the Battle of Agincourt.

Although the garrison may attempt to send messages through the English lines requesting urgent relief, encouraged by the umpire to devise cunning schemes or diversions for this purpose, and may receive replies, no actual relieving army will appear. Messages the umpire determines would fall into enemy hands will by given to the English players.

Once a practicable breach has – in the opinion of the master engineer – been made, by bombardment or mining, King Henry will summon the town to surrender. His objective is to secure Harfleur quickly, before relief can arrive, with the least possible casualties and damage – so the town can be garrisoned and defended against French forces. He can afford to offer generous terms. The commander of the garrison, de Gaucourt, will be determined to hold out as long as he can, but will only refuse to treat if he is sure that his forces can repulse an attempt to storm the town. Negotiations may be conducted by the players, face-to-face, while the umpire records the number of days that elapse, informing each side secretly of the number of troops fit for service, their morale and the supply situation, changes to which may alter their negotiating position. Victory is achieved by the English if Harfleur accepts terms no more generous or harsher than those originally granted by the same date as, or earlier than, the historical surrender. The French win if they can secure better terms by the same date, or hold out longer before accepting those obtained historically.

Act II: 'We Band of Brothers' Council of War

The scene shifts from the English siege lines to the King's War Council. In this Act, the umpire plays Henry V and the players the principal English commanders – the Dukes of Gloucester and York, the Earl of Oxford, Lord Camoys, Sir Gilbert Umfraville, Sir John Cornwall, John Holland and the commander of the English garrison of Harfleur, the Earl of Dorset. Their task is to discuss the future course of the campaign and advise the King. It is now late in the year to undertake a campaign, so the English have only three choices:

1 to leave a strong garrison in Harfleur and ship the rest of the army, greatly reduced by sickness, to England for the winter;
2 to establish a Harfleur Pale, like that at Calais; or
3 to undertake a march to Calais, a chevauchée to demonstrate that the King can go where he will in the lands he claims as his own.

Each player will be given a Personal Briefing explaining his character's views on the possible strategies above; in addition, some characters may have their private rivalries or loyalties, which may outweigh strategic considerations when it is time to vote, so that, for example, no character will vote

the same way as his deadly rival, while others may be open to persuasion by debate. The King will act as chairman.

Victory is achieved either by persuading the War Council to support one's favoured strategy or – if the King chooses to overrule the Council's recommendations – by being a dissenter who voted in favour of that choice afterwards made by the King. Conversely, the minority who both lose the debate and support a view contrary to that of the King will suffer a severe loss of prestige and Royal confidence. Players will also gain prestige for entering into the spirit of their roles and acting in a manner appropriate to their characters. Prestige points could be awarded to rank the players' performances in the War Council and determine their roles or combat ratings in the final battle. The King will, of course, reject his War Council's advice if it does not recommend a chevauchée – though this should be concealed from the players – in order that the game may follow the historical course of the campaign.

A similar game could be created to portray the discussions of the French commanders, though problems might be encountered in endeavouring to avoid changing history!

Act III: Chevauchée – The March to Calais

In *The Agincourt War*, Lieutenant-Colonel Burne suggests that Henry V may have had a map of the region, perhaps even the identical one used by his great-grandfather, Edward III. If the game organizer accepts this proposition, he must remember that mediaeval maps or army itineraries were not drawn according to the principles of modern cartography, and produce a suitably illuminated, naively executed document to 'assist' the players. Towns will be indicated by vignettes; distances in terms of day's marches. The English commander will issue his marching orders to the umpire, who will record the army's actual progress on his accurately scaled master-map and impart appropriate news of the enemy – either pre-programmed to manoeuvre historically, or played by another participant using a similarly archaic, but more accurate, map – and intelligence of the countryside through which the English army passes.

Alternatively, King Henry, if not permitted a map, must rely upon local guides to discover the most practicable route to the next town or river crossing. To represent the hazards of using such guides, the King or his commanders must select them from cards showing portraits and brief descriptions – the accuracy of which the players will have to guess! – of prospective guides. The umpire has a definitive list of all the guides, indicating each one's reliability, which will determine the English army's actual progress: incompetent guides may take the army to its desired destination by a roundabout route, losing much valuable time, or become completely lost! Treacherous guides may lead the English towards the gathering French army or to fords which they know to be defended, for example; while reliable guides will take the most speedy route. Reconnaissance by both sides may be simulated by placing overlays, in which circular holes have been cut to represent the scouts' range of vision from a vantage point, such as a hill-top, or across open country, over a pictorial rendition of the terrain. As the scouts ride onward, the umpire advances the overlay so that the hole shows what they can see at any one time. Players may not make notes or sketches until the end of their reconnaissance – after all, most mediaeval soldiers would have been only semi-literate at best, and untrained in the art of military sketching. The use of modern Ordnance Survey or tactical symbols must be forbidden!

The English army begins the march with eight days' supply of food (though the soldiers no doubt either consumed their rations more quickly than their commanders would have wished, or jettisoned what they considered to be an unnecessarily heavy burden, as did the Redcoats of the Peninsular War) which may be exhausted earlier than the players anticipate, at the umpire's discretion. Arrangements must then be made to requisition supplies from the local inhabitants, or troops dispersed to forage, if the army is not to suffer losses from exhaustion or starvation.

The English objective is to reach Calais without being intercepted, or to have to offer battle no earlier than was the case in the historical campaign, without losing a great number of men from the hardships of the march. The French aim to bring the English to battle quickly with their main army, or to harry them across country to Calais, inflicting heavier losses from attrition and the capture of stragglers than were actually suffered. The umpire will, if at all possible, contrive an interception at some stage so that the final Act may be performed . . .

Act IV: Saint Crispin's Day – The Battle of Agincourt

It is extremely unlikely that using the historical forces and terrain as a scenario for a conventional wargame will result in a convincing recreation of Agincourt, however much the participants may enjoy such games. Hindsight will surely dissuade the players commanding the French from committing their men-at-arms to an attack in the manner of their historical counterparts. However, those who wish to choose this approach will find it easy to recreate the terrain of the battlefield by spreading a thick cloth or blanket over miscellaneous household flotsam to form the shallow depression between the two armies and the slopes which fell away on either flank, and placing model trees or clumps of lichen to indicate the edges of the woods surrounding the villages of Agincourt and Tramecourt on opposite sides of the table top.

Suitable figures are available in all the popular sizes for wargaming: 25mm, 15mm and 6mm from numerous manufacturers. The game organizer will also be able to select from several sets of commercial rules, of which the Wargames Research Group's Seventh Edition Ancient Period rules and those published by Newbury Rules are most likely to be familiar already to prospective players. Such rules tend to be rather complex and to produce slow-moving games when administered by only two opposing players: they are best suited to a multi-player game in which participants command individual 'battles' or divisions of the rival armies. A much simpler, but very stylized, set of rules, which would suit two players and small-scale figures, is 'De Bellis Antiquitatis' or DBA for short, published by the Wargames Research Group. These rules will enable even inexperienced wargamers to fight a complete battle to a finish within two hours, and would be ideal for those with no previous knowledge of the period.

A radically different approach would seek to recreate the individual's experience and perception of Agincourt by concentrating upon hand-to-hand combat between the French men-at-arms and their English opponents (both men-at-arms and archers) assuming that both armies deploy and act historically. In such a game each player would take the role of an individual man-at-arms or peasant infantryman; his objectives would be, first, to survive (or, in the case of a nobleman only, to achieve glory in battle, even at the cost of his life); to defeat opponents in personal combat; and to take prisoners for subsequent ransom. Non-played characters on either side would be moved by a team of umpires, who would also control such figures when engaged in personal combat with players (combat between non-played characters would be resolved by a 'sudden-death' comparison of die rolls). The game could accommodate as many wargamers as wished to participate – the more the better!

Such a game would consist of a display of 25mm or 15mm figures on a model terrain to the same scale as the miniature troops. Players would move their own personality figures and accompanying retinues; umpires would control the rest. Random blows, wounds or death inflicted by archery would be resolved by die rolls, administered by umpires, individuals wearing armour having a greater chance of surviving unscathed than peasants. The behaviour of horses would also be determined by the umpires, though mounted men-at-arms who beat their assigned Horsemanship Rating with the die could bring their mounts back under control – at least until struck by another shaft! – and continue to move their figures themselves. Players whose horses fell, stampeded or impaled themselves on the archers' stakes would draw chance cards or throw dice and consult a table to discover their fate.

Personal combat involving at least one played character would be resolved using an adaptation of the 'Chivalry' system published by Games Workshop in *White Dwarf*, number 130, October 1990. This system requires two decks of cards: Attack Cards, which indicate the areas of the body aimed at; and Defence Cards showing the areas protected by the defender's reactions. After dicing to determine which is the Attacker, the players draw cards from one or both decks up to the number of their initial Combat Values. The Attacker plays one of his cards face up, whereupon the Defender must produce the appropriate counter from his hand or – if he has no suitable Defence Card – take a chance and draw the top card from the Defence deck to block the blow; if he fails to do so, he is wounded and his hand is reduced by the number of cards equivalent to the severity, shown as a number rating, of the attack. If the Defender does parry or dodge the blow successfully, he becomes the Attacker in the next round of combat. Play continues until one player is either incapacitated by wounds and unable to defend himself or killed outright by certain deadly attacks. This system, in its present form, is designed for combat between evenly matched mediaeval knights but could easily be adapted with a little ingenuity to cater for encounters between men-at-arms on horseback and on foot, and archers armed with daggers, axes and mallets. Fatigue could be simulated by reducing the hand by one card for a given number of turns of combat; armoured men would have little chance of being killed outright, but might be beaten to the ground, or trip in the press of combatants, and then be at the mercy of a *coup de grâce* from a dagger through the visor or armpit; archers could be allowed more Defence Cards to represent their greater agility, but fewer Attack Cards than men-at-arms; individual nobles could have different Combat Values, and so on. Players unable to defend themselves might cry 'Quarter!' and thus surrender for subsequent ransom.

Victory conditions for English archers might include amassing the highest sum of money in potential ransoms and looted armour or weapons! The cunning player who takes the role of King Henry in such a game will, no doubt, negotiate appropriate contracts with those commanding his miniature troops, whereby he will take a share of any ransoms they may secure from prisoners. Mercenary wargamers may care to recast the whole campaign to emphasise the financial aspects of mediaeval campaigning!